CRISIS NOW

CRISIS

NOW

by

JAMES M. GAVIN

in collaboration with

Arthur T. Hadley

RANDOM HOUSE / NEW YORK

FIRST PRINTING

Copyright © 1968 by
James M. Gavin and Arthur T. Hadley

All rights reserved under International and Pan-American
Copyright Conventions. Published in the United States by
Random House, Inc., New York, and simultaneously in
Canada by Random House of Canada Limited, Toronto.

LIBRARY OF CONGRESS CATALOG CARD NUMBER: 68-14522

Manufactured in the United States of America

Designed by Carl Weiss

PREFACE

Several years ago it seemed to me the quality of American life had begun to alter. We no longer faced and tried to understand our problems. Instead we hid from them in a variety of ways; and when they finally forced themselves on us, we had no answer but past solutions. In short, we were not living in the present.

I felt that the country had never faced a more dangerous and at the same moment a more challenging time. That either we had to begin to try and solve the grievous ills that affected our society, understand the modern meaning of strategy and make this understanding manifest in our policies, or we would suffer critically.

As our crisis continued, I began to consider ways in which I might do something. Twice in the past I had written a book as one method of bringing solutions then relatively unknown before as wide a number of people as possible. Though occupied with a variety of other tasks, I kept the idea of a book in the back of my mind for about two years. By last summer it seemed to me that the need to speak out, to try to turn the country around, had become intense. I resolved to make the time to write a book. This decision made, I looked around for someone to help me.

About twenty years before, I had encountered an eager, young newspaper reporter in the E wing of the Pentagon. He was then writing on military affairs and for the "Periscope" page of *Newsweek*. I talked to him briefly and found it a fascinating experience. "Periscope" at that time was being troublesome to many in Washington. It had shown a facility for coming up week after week with a great deal of information that was closely held in Washington circles. The newspaperman was Arthur Hadley; and after I got to know him better I understood why "Periscope" was doing so well. He not only had a rare capacity to get the facts, but an unusual ability to analyze and on the basis of his analysis to anticipate what might be next.

I had just finished a course at our Nuclear Weapons School and had attended some tests in the Pacific; and had begun to have my first doubts about the growing reliance upon the "big bombs" to solve all of our problems. It seemed to me that in a democracy the application of military force should be as flexible as democracy itself, and that in international affairs any punishment America meted out to an aggressor must be tailored to fit the crime. A Hitler would have found big bombs a fine exclusive weapon with which to solve all his problems; but the President of the United States needed a variety of solutions.

I was a lonesome voice at that time, but I soon found intellectual company in Arthur Hadley, for he too shared my feelings about the sterility and inadequacy of "massive retaliation at a time and a place of our choosing." Later I served two years in NATO; and upon returning to

Washington I resumed my friendship with Hadley and spent many absorbing hours discussing the broad terms of national policy.

Our recent discussions have been on national strategy and the significance of Vietnam. Again we have found ourselves in almost complete agreement as to what should be done, both in America and abroad. We see Vietnam as poisoning our society at home and causing us to make serious mistakes in the conduct of our international affairs abroad. The Soviet penetration of the Middle East, the ill will in NATO over our Vietnam policy, our marginal ability to deal with situations that arise in other parts of the world, and our near paralysis before our domestic crisis, all relate to our Vietnam involvement. Since we had so often discussed these matters, I asked Hadley to work with me on the book. This is that book.

In the preparation a great many others have generously contributed their time and thoughts. Many of these are presently in the government and asked that they be not mentioned. But while respecting their wishes I would like nevertheless to thank them warmly. In Cambridge a number of people at Arthur D. Little, Incorporated, and at the Organization for Social and Technical Innovation have contributed to my knowledge of urban problems not only in the course of writing this book but over an extended period of time. Their learning and insight have been of great help. Peter Labovitz of ADL and Donald A. Schon of OSTI in particular aided in both the preparation and criticism of the manuscript. The Honorable Teodoro Moscoso, special adviser to the assistant secretary of state for inter-American affairs, has generously taken time to guide me through the often neglected subject of Latin America.

In locating and researching the necessary facts both in libraries and on the ground, I have had the help of Maude Dorr, Nancy Hoepli and Kay Manion. Dorothy Littlefield typed the many drafts of the manuscript with speed and accuracy. I am most grateful to them all.

JAMES M. GAVIN
BOSTON, 1967

*　　*　　*

When a prominent figure produces a book in an election year, the suspicion often arises that the book is not his own. That he merely took some past speeches (perhaps ghostwritten themselves) and some clippings; and told someone to produce a book. This did not happen here. This is James Gavin's book. Those who have read his previous books and articles in magazines ranging from the *Atlantic Monthly* to the *Saturday Review* know he stands alone as both a thinker and a writer. I have merely tried to lift from him some of the pressures of time. The credit he so publicly gives me measures his generosity rather than my contribution. His kindness equals his legendary courage.

A. T. HADLEY
WEST TISBURY, 1967

CONTENTS

Truth can never be told so as to
be understood, and not be believed.

—WILLIAM BLAKE

I

THE CONTINUING

REVOLUTION

America is in crisis. Two years ago when I first used these words I found few who agreed with me. Now talk of the American crisis rises everywhere. Some minimize it; some maximize it. Some claim we will get through easily, while others wring their hands and prophesy doom. A few even try to understand how we got here and why. But practically no one any longer denies that we have reached a critical period in our national life.

I believe we face choices unparalleled in our history and that how we deal with our problems will have profound consequences for ourselves and the world. I hope that even those who disagree with one or more of my strategies and solutions will find their knowledge of America's present deepened by reading this book.

To find the issues behind our crisis is not difficult. America's problems explode at us daily, not just secondhand but touch close in our lives. And their violence is unpleasant for all, fatal for some.

In the multitude of problems that concern us, two are most immediate: the war in Vietnam and the disintegration of our cities. Both these crises are desperate. In both, men die. The war in Vietnam would seem to be the more urgent because a military disaster there—either general defeat or escalation to total war—would so convulse the United States that the chance to solve the problems of our cities would vanish. But complex as the Vietnam problem is, it seems to me, for reasons this book will outline, to be the simpler of the two. At least the entrances to that labyrinth, the paths that need to be taken, are visible.

Customarily the disintegration of our cities and the war in Vietnam are viewed as two separate issues, and they are felt to stem from different causes. The only thread between them is believed to be the tragic one: they are happening to ourselves and at the same time. To me, however, they are both part of the same disturbing pattern of change which disarranges other portions of our lives. This change is the often cited but seldom understood "scientific revolution." By the scientific revolution I mean not only the new concepts and inventions themselves but their direct and indirect effect on our lives.

Even as the Industrial Revolution dominated and shaped the eighteenth and nineteenth centuries, so the scientific revolution molds this present era. And our failure to master the far-reaching consequences of this revolution has created a world threatened by many ills, great and small—from the polluted air we breathe and the contaminated water we drink, the untested pills we swallow, the automobiles that choke our cities, the unemployment caused by computers and automation, and the population explosions in a world already over-crowded, to the effect of atomic weapons and other new military concepts on our foreign and military policy.

All around us the scientific revolution has created a wide gap between the world as it is and the world as we believe it to be. This distortion of our vision, this gap in our knowledge, makes it close to impossible for us to solve our problems. For they cannot be solved until they are seen and understood.

Because of this knowledge gap our crises take us by surprise, and we flail at their tentacles without under-standing their basic causes. For example, we allow our-selves to believe that riots in our cities will be solved by shooting rioters or that the Vietnamese war can be ended by bombing North Vietnamese. Neither is true. Unless we understand the causes of our problems and their size we cannot take the necessary first steps toward their solution. As indeed too often we have not.

THE KNOWLEDGE GAP

Sometimes complex concepts are best approached by using simple illustrations. Here follow several small emergencies created by the scientific revolution. These happened because we were unprepared for the com-plexity of that revolution and could not see the obvious in front of us. These events are not as horrendous as the issues just mentioned; but they brought needless suffer-ing and even death to an unfortunately large number of people. And if we fail in the small things, how shall we handle the large?

On March 18, 1967 the oil tanker *Torrey Canyon* ran on the rocks of Seven Stones Reef off Cornwall, England. Into the ocean from the ship's broken hull poured 60,000 tons of fuel oil. The result was economic disaster for a wide area, not just in Great Britain but across the channel in France. Beaches were polluted, fishing industries all but destroyed, and the ecological balance of the ocean over a large area was profoundly altered.

Neither the scientific nor the industrial community, nor the governments of Britain and France had any solutions to offer other than hoping the wind would shift. (And praying for the wind to shift has ever been a precarious basis for human planning.) The *Torrey Canyon* disaster caused enormous damage. Yet the oil-carrying capacity of the *Torrey Canyon*, 120,000 tons, is small compared to other giants plying today's oceans with capacities of over 200,000 tons. And on the drawing board are vessels capable of carrying 500,000 plus tons.

The opportunity for a major disaster was right there, sailing around, completely visible. The ship had been created by science and technology which invented and perfected the special metals, pumps, and navigational aides; and also created the economic organization and world markets that made the tanker desirable. Yet no one had foreseen the disaster. Or taken the necessary steps to mitigate the results of such a tanker breaking up.

In another area there is the disturbing story of deformities and deaths of infants resulting from the use of the tranquilizer thalidomide by pregnant women. Investigation made clear that the drug had been placed on the European market without proper testing. In the testimony that followed the uncovering of the causes of the tragedy the methods for the licensing of new drugs were shown to be inadequate, and though they have been improved subsequently, inadequacies remain. Yet the scientific revolution continues to flood the market with new drugs and other like products without thorough testing.

Yet another tragedy is in the making. Some dark, smoky day a great many people in one of our major cities, say New York or Los Angeles, are going to die of air pollution. Then everyone will scream for the villain, who, it will have to be admitted, will be ourselves.

And ahead lie even more difficult problems. For, as a recent editorial in the magazine *Science* pointed out, before long ". . . man may be able to program his own cells with synthetic information long before he will be able to assess adequately the long-term consequences of such alterations, long before he will be able to formulate goals, and long before he can resolve the ethical and moral problems which will be raised."

FIRST CAUSES

To find the scientific revolution a major cause of both the Vietnamese war and our crumbling cities may seem far-fetched. But it is my firm belief that this basic theme, among others, links them both.

The Vietnamese war is a specific example of the general problem of limited war. And the whole nature, possibilities, problems and dangers of limited war appeared with the scientific fact of the first nuclear explosion. With the advent of nuclear weapons the old Clausewitzian orthodoxy that war is a continuation of politics by other means has disappeared. Also, no longer true is the attractive idea that something shining and definite called "victory" can be achieved by destroying enough people and property. For since a nuclear holocaust must be avoided, it follows that a primary objective of both sides in a limited war should be to keep such a war limited. And this means limited in duration as well as in weapons used and area fought over.

The problem of our disintegrating cities is more complex. But a majority of the factors underlying urban unrest spring from our inability to understand and cope with the technological application of science to our society. The depressed urban Negro rightly feels closed out from our culture, for automation and mechanization have abolished even those unskilled jobs into which he had hitherto been segregated. And lacking education, and more importantly, the incentives of opportunity, he finds the technical skills that are the keys to the kingdom of affluence more and more difficult to acquire.

At the same time such factors as food and data processing, rapid transport and communications, the need for all sections of our increasingly complex industrial society to live in close contact with each other, combine to accelerate the need and conditions for urban growth. Pile on top of this the population explosion resulting from the progress of medical and nutritional science and the migration off the farm as the result of new chemical fertilizers and the mechanization of agriculture and you have some of the beginnings of the urban problem. Science and technology created this vast inhumanness. Now those same forces must be harnessed to humanize and make livable again the world around us.

Marshall McLuhan has remarked: "Very few men look at the present with a present eye, they tend to miss the present by translating it into the past, seeing it through a rear-view mirror." This is all too true. We cannot, of course, determine where we are without some reference to the past. But we must view the past too with a present eye. And unfortunately, the more successful the past the greater the temptation to merely look in the mirror.

When business is prospering and military and foreign affairs are stable, as was the situation in the period between World War I and the depression or between Korea and Vietnam, the resistance to change is of course much greater than in a time of national emergency or grave social upheaval. Look at the social revolution that took place in this country between 1932 and 1940—and at the social and economic chaos that preceded it. On March 4, 1933, when President Franklin Delano Roosevelt was inaugurated, our nation was in dire straits. As historian Arthur M. Schlesinger Jr. has described it: "The national income was less than half of what it had been four short years before. Nearly thirteen million Americans—about one-quarter of the labor force—were desperately seeking jobs. The machinery for sheltering and feeding the unemployed was breaking down everywhere under the growing burden. And a few hours before, in the early morning before the inauguration every bank in America had locked its doors."

The nation had taken the soundness of its institutions for granted for too long. Social change was urgently needed. And in that time of economic collapse people were willing to accept the fresh ideas, approaches and actions of the New Deal. To say that we are in an equal crisis today is to understate our present problem by several orders of magnitude. In the words of the late President Kennedy: "It is the fate of this generation . . . to live with a struggle we did not start in a world we did not make. But the pressures of life are not always distributed by choice. And while no nation has ever faced such a challenge, no nation has ever been so ready to seize the burden and the glory of freedom."

But even with ability to understand the processes and effects of the scientific revolution; to see where we are; we still are not guaranteed success. For not only are new social and political ideas scarce, but in equally desperate short supply is the ability to nourish them, to bring them about, translate them from words, graphs and figures into the hard framework of human reality. New ideas unfortunately do not flourish like radishes but have to be nurtured like orchids. With men and institutions by nature conservative and resistant to change, only the expert can make the new idea effective; see that it is not merely thought, but is used for the benefit of society.

Machiavelli, no mean student of the process of change, expressed the problem in these words: "There is nothing more difficult to carry out, or more doubtful of success, nor more dangerous to handle, than to initiate a new order of things." Politicians and people tend to leave well enough alone. Unfortunately neither in Vietnam nor our cities do we have a well enough that can be left alone. Either we find new ideas and use them or the scientific revolution will continue to push us into less understandable wars and an endless succession of long, hot summers, each more torrid than the last.

THE MANAGEMENT
OF COMPLEXITY

But the outlook need not be one of total gloom. For Americans have developed the skills, techniques, and mental attitude necessary to solve their major problems once they see them clearly. In our giant industries, and in government too, we have in part mastered the process of taking new developments or ideas and successfully controlling them. Economists have shown us that we have created a new form of organization, the gigantic corporation, one of whose functions is the handling of new ideas without the wild fluctuations of risk. America excels in its ability to manage and organize complexity, and more than any other nation it has developed the new skills necessary to handle the problems of the second half of this century. This is what gives me hope. If we can understand our problems and face them, I am certain we can help ourselves.

Generals who find in their military experience analogies to civilian problems are often suspect. Be that as it may,

I believe the creation of American airborne forces, with which I was intimately associated during World War II, indicates ways in which we can handle many of our problems today.

The United States began the experiment of dropping men and weapons by parachute in 1923. But during the lean peacetime years progress was slow. In the summer of 1940 the first experimental parachute platoon (less than fifty men) was organized. I was teaching tactics at West Point at the time and it seemed to me that the tactics of the blitzkrieg and the use of an ever-larger scale of armored formations would not be enough, and that we would have to find a new dimension of warfare. I therefore obtained an assignment with the parachute troops, and after qualifying as a jumper was put in charge of plans, training, and the development of doctrine for this new type of force.

It was a good place to be. For under the stress of war the military establishment was desperately looking for new ideas and doctrines, but there were many who did not give the airborne much of a future. I was told at one time that the United States would never use more than a few platoons of paratroopers because there would never be enough airfields to launch anything so large as a division. Yet three years later, as senior airborne adviser to General Eisenhower prior to D-Day, I was planning the landing of three airborne divisions for the night before and in the early hours of D-Day. And by the war's end we had five airborne divisions, an airborne corps and the First Allied Airborne Army.

After the war in the course of a conversation with a high-ranking Russian parachute officer in Berlin I asked why the Russians had not used their airborne troops on a more major scale and in a more decisive way. He replied that they just had never found it possible to organize fully all the men, airplanes, and vehicles necessary for massive operations. I then realized that our greatest achievement had not been the development of a new concept but the technique of management. We knew from the beginning that we wanted our units to be decisive, to operate as large, well-managed forces. We had to solve problems of communications, new tactical procedures, develop new aircraft, devise new troop formations and weapons. But above all we had to coordinate all this, and to develop an organization to adapt and direct the new science and technology.

It struck me then that the type of planning and management that we were doing in the Army was new—new both in its scope and diversity and in its pioneering use of the latest scientific advice and equipment, such as systems analysis, operational research, data control. Since there was no word to describe what we were doing I privately gave it the name technoplanning. In later years, dealing with private industry, I found that the major corporations were also engaging in technoplanning. And recently Professor John Kenneth Galbraith has brilliantly identified a whole vast stratum of America as the "Technostructure," the chief business of which is the preparation and execution of complex plans.

. . .

The ability to handle large problems is abundantly present here in America. But first, I repeat, we must recognize and understand the problems.

This book was written in response to the interest generated by some of the solutions to certain current American problems that I have proposed in books, articles and in testimony before Congress. I make no claim in a book this size to total wizardry. Nor does it take twenty-twenty vision to see that America has some major problems and note what they are. But it seems to me that very few people have been looking at our cities, our military establishment, the war in Vietnam, our pockets of poverty and our race relations in a true way. Few have seen them as part of a new rapidly changing system created by the scientific revolution. I have tried to see our present crises not through a glass darkly, but face to face. In offering a few strategies to get us turned around and to deal with our crisis in a modern, scientific way, I hope I can influence people to make the commitment to change now. We should not fear change. It is pointless to. For in this period, change will occur at an increasing rate. If we look around us we can see clear evidence of this already. What we must fear is that our situation will change for the worse—in Vietnam or our cities—and we, apathetic or not understanding why, will be unable to reverse the processes of deterioration.

There are many things we should be doing to make certain that we control this future, that it does not merely burst on us like an unforecast hurricane. To take a specific instance, I am greatly concerned that we have no cabinet secretary for science. There is no one with prestige and statutory authority, not merely to distribute the ever-growing federal funds going into research, but to exercise some direction and control over that research—and equally important, to anticipate our needs and initiate new research. For all our problems presently occur in the context of the scientific frontier—just as in the nineteenth century they occurred in the context of the physical frontier.

If we handle our natural resources wisely—especially the abilities and brains of our people—then the scientific revolution in its most beneficial sense will serve both our domestic and foreign interests. If we waste our resources —waste the abilities of any portion of our people—then all our other problems will multiply.

Our future in this period of expanding knowledge and technology is at least as challenging as when our physical frontier moved west. Only this time there is no peaceful eastern seaboard to which we can retreat. We are all pioneers. As a nation now, we are as home-steaders then. Either we master the environment around us or we succumb. Fortunately, men are responsive to challenge. Indeed, as Toynbee has pointed out and an-thropologists have documented, man does best when con-fronted by a degree of challenge.

These lines by Walt Whitman have always seemed to me to describe the times in which I have found my-self.

> Long, too long America
> Traveling roads all even and peaceful you learned
>   from joys and prosperity only.

[19]

But now, ah now, to learn from the crisis of anguish,
advancing, grappling with direct fate and
recoiling not.

II

THE CHANGED NATURE
OF WAR AND STRATEGY

I would rather that the organization of this book placed the chapters on America's urban crisis and the human environment before those on strategy, war and Vietnam. In complexity, difficulty and danger to ourselves I believe our domestic crisis is our most important problem. Yet Vietnam is a roadblock in both our thoughts and national energies. We seem unable to give solutions to our domestic problems more than lip service until we have begun a resolution of that war. Therefore it seemed wise to deal first with the specific problem of Vietnam.

And since Vietnam is a special example of war in general and limited war in particular, it cannot be understood without some idea of how warfare has been profoundly altered by nuclear energy—another aspect of the scientific revolution.

Before analyzing war and strategy in the nuclear age, I want to make one point totally clear. I am not advocating war of any size as a means of settling national disputes. Indeed, as my public testimony and writing show, I have been struggling all my life to see that wars did not happen—and if they did happen, that they were isolated rapidly, kept limited, and held to where they could be settled by diplomacy.

A psychiatrist helps a human being to lead a whole life by examining with him the dark side of his nature. In such a spirit it is sometimes necessary to examine war. For if we do not understand the nature of strategy and war in the postnuclear age, peace and national greatness will escape us no matter how earnestly we wish for them. There is no use searching for peace with the wrong tools in the wrong place.

War, science and organization have always gone hand in hand. Indeed food gathering, religion and war would appear to be man's three oldest collective undertakings. No matter whether the war was just or unjust, important or trivial, to those involved in that moment of history the battle seemed vital. They strained their social organization to the uttermost to achieve victory.

WARFARE IN HISTORY

From the rough charge of clan and tribe, through phalanx, cavalry sweeps, and blockading naval squadrons, to price controls, materials allocation, surtaxes, and total mobilization, man has structured and ordered his society and military forces for battle in units of ever-increasing size and complexity. At the same time he has turned to science to give him weapons of ever-greater strength. Iron swords to break the bronze, animal sinews to hurl weapons further than thrown stones. Archimedes harnessing the sun's energy through lenses to fire the Roman ships at Syracuse. Iron gave way to steel, oil replaced coal, Greek fire was dwarfed by gunpowder, gunpowder yielded to TNT, still the scientists searched on for new sources of energy that would increase the killing power of their particular side.

Finally, using the knowledge and tools provided by the scientific revolution, scientists generated here on earth the explosive power comparable to that taking place on the sun itself. The search had finally ended. The theoretical limits of destructive power had been reached. New ways might be found to place the nuclear explosive on target more efficiently; engineering and chemical refinements might slightly increase the power of a bomb of a given weight. But such improvements are relative compared to the quantum jump in destructive power from TNT to nuclear fusion. Before, we thought in pounds. Now mankind has learned a new word: "megatons."

When "Thin Boy," the first nuclear weapon, was detonated over Hiroshima at 8:15 A.M., August 6, 1945, the world changed. Many have said this. Only a few have thought and acted on the implications of the change. The scientists who developed the bomb had forecast accurately the nature of the explosion that would occur. But even they had but dimly envisioned the changes in warfare and diplomacy that were to follow. And the reactions of generals, admirals, diplomats and politicians to nuclear weapons were confused, slow and unfortunately often uninformed and wrong. And I question how much we understand the psychological changes that must have occurred in mankind as a result of living under the threat of nuclear extinction.

THE NUCLEAR AGE

Before Hiroshima, war and strategy were comparatively stereotyped and simple in character. The building blocks of national power were understandable entities: so many battleships, so many metric tons of steel production, so many divisions in the field, so many in the reserve, this nation and that nation bound by ties of blood and alliance. Nations who coveted what others had, or wanted to regain what they believed was rightfully theirs, made treaties, fabricated the latest weapons, mobilized and maneuvered their fleets and divisions. All this was national *strategy*. If a nation was successful in its strategy its adversaries gave in and it obtained its way by politics and diplomacy. If the nation had miscalculated or its adversaries refused to back down, then the nation went to war. This is of course an oversimplification, but in outline it is correct.

From this scheme of things rose two basic postulates of strategy and warfare. Both of these still dominate much of our thinking, though both have been proved invalid since Hiroshima. Before the nature of modern strategy can be outlined and the needs and dangers of modern warfare understood, it is necessary to examine and refute these two myths.

The first of these is the oft-repeated dictum of the German military strategist Karl von Clausewitz that war is a continuation of politics by other means. In the Clausewitzian orthodoxy war is seen as a definite state of affairs apart from the life of a nation. There is peace. And there is war. The two are distinct. In war, power is applied until one or the other nation yields. Then the world reverts to a period of peace. Diplomacy and statecraft once again become the paramount strategy for adjusting disputes.

I believe that by now most thoughtful people recognize as obsolete for our time this simplistic view of peace and war as two distinct times in a nation's life. There is economic war, cold war, espionage, guerrilla war, limited war, the war of ideas, etc. The "war" we came close to at the time of the Cuban missile crisis is vastly different from the war we now fight in Vietnam. A nation faces challenges to its power and exerts its influence on others in a variety of shifting ways. War and peace blend.

Strategy is complex. We do not suddenly shift gears and go from being at "peace" to driving all out for "victory."

We no longer have then a distinct state of war or any definite boundary between war and peace. Rather we have a long and continuous spectrum of national life in which peace merges imperceptibly into war and war itself slowly escalates to total nuclear holocaust. Having understood this, we can now examine the second, even more pervasive myth.

The second myth holds that the proper way for a nation to prosecute the distinct state of war, i.e., to wage war, is to throw all the power it has at the enemy, including nuclear weapons, until the enemy gives in. "There is no substitute for victory" is a popular slogan used by those who think in these prenuclear-age terms. This view springs from the incorrect assumption that war is a part of national life distinct from peace. But far more seriously it imperils us all because it stems from the failure to understand the change in warfare brought about by nuclear weapons.

The truth of the nuclear age is—and we may all sleep easier because more and more people are coming to understand this truth—that both we and the Soviet Union possess the power to totally destroy each other. Experts may quibble about whether the degree of destruction will be 83 per cent or 92 per cent depending on the weather pattern at H-hour, the height of burst and who struck first. I am reasonably expert in this field myself, and I am willing to stand behind the adjective "total" in describing the destruction both we and the Soviets could visit upon the other. The colossal might of thermonuclear weapons, plus the very effectiveness of both the strategic air force and strategic missile systems, prevents their use in other than total war.

War is violent and volatile. At any moment, even if both sides are trying to keep the war limited, it may escalate sharply toward nuclear holocaust. With the threat of such total destruction ever present it follows that the primary task of the military should be to keep any wars that may occur as limited as possible—and this means limited in time also, something the Vietnamese war has not been. And a primary responsibility of American political leaders should be: first, to provide the guidelines under which the military can limit the war, and second, through rigorous diplomatic negotiation to provide the means by which the war can be ended.

In summary then, we live in a world where "peace," "war," and "total war" merge imperceptibly into each other. Nations now apply their power throughout the world in a variety of ways, from feeding the starving to shooting bullets. With the threat of nuclear destruction ever present both politician and soldier should strive to sharply limit any such wars as may occur. Within the limits the war may be violent. Both Korea and Vietnam have seen plenty of dying. But to prevent escalation to total nuclear war the limits must be understood and maintained.

With these two myths cleared away we can now examine the changed nature of strategy.

STRATEGY TODAY

What is strategy? Strategy is the way a nation applies its power to maintain its existence in the world. A wise nation keeps its strategy as peaceful as possible, not only because war is wasteful and often self-defeating, but also because, in the words of the Eddic bard, "When the outcome goes to the sword's edge, fate's slippery." And he sang long before the possibility of thermo-nuclear immolation.

In this postnuclear age I see four main elements of strategy: economics, science-technology, ideas and finally military power. I would like to examine each of these briefly. To those who are experts in the field I apologize for the brevity of this outline, which however may be generally useful because the subject is still little under-stood. And knowledge is essential if we are to debate our national problems intelligently.

Economics The industrial base of a nation, the ability of a people to organize production efficiently and make weapons, has been recognized as an important element of national power long before the Romans fought for Cornwall's tin. But in recent decades economics has had a more direct effect on strategy. Through foreign aid, disaster relief and international trade, America makes other nations conscious of her power. The economic slogan of the eighteenth century was "trade followed the flag"; in our age, the flag follows trade. The emerg-ing nations realize this full well; so they desperately search for loans and credits with which to build heavy industry and thus pursue their strategy of independence.

In the realm of economic strategy I find the fall of Premier Khrushchev highly significant. Khrushchev's failure was not in the Cuban missile crisis. That was a small tactical error from which, after his defeat by President Kennedy, he recovered quickly. His basic failure was his inability to make good on his challenge to the United States: "Let us compete in the realm of trade and we will see who wins." He set his country lofty goals in economic growth, crop production, consumer goods. He promised lavish economic aid around the world. In all of these aims he fell short. And the world knew it. Similarly the economic failure of China's "great leap forward" and the excess of Mao Tse-tung's Cultural Revolution have as much if not more to do with her declining influence among her neighbors than the presence of a U.S. fleet in Asiatic waters.

I believe it follows from this that the efficiency of our economy at home will have as much effect on our position in the world as anything else that we do. I do not wish to sound materialistic or isolationist and imply that a lavish supply of domestic goods is everything. But the ability of our economy to continue to cope successfully with the complexities of the scientific revolution and provide an increasingly better standard of living for all our people will have a major effect on our standing as a world power.

Science-technology This combined field is vital in the struggle among nations for strategic dominance. Again I do not refer to the effect alone, great though it is, of science and technology on weapons production, but to the other ways in which science-technology influences our national power. Perhaps the most dramatic of these is the space race.

There are some who protest that the space race is an area of competition we should stay out of. However, the boost to Russian prestige when the Soviets orbited the first satellite, and our own elation when John Glenn circled the earth or when the first close-up views of Mars were radioed back, should convince all but the most confirmed opponents of the program that we should be in the race to stay. In the space race the various elements of national strategy merge, as they so often do. If we manage our economy wisely we should be able to continue our foreign aid, increase our affluence at home, attack the problems in our cities, and still provide the economic base for our scientific-technical competition in space. Of course, in part our economic growth rests upon the proper application of science and technology to industry.

We must realize that for both the developed nations of Europe and the emerging nations around the globe our scientific-technological skill is at the same time a source of strength and a threat. Europeans grow emotional on the subject of the "brain drain" (as more and more of their scientists leave for America) and the technological dominance of the United States. I believe their fears are exaggerated, but we should be aware that they exist. We must wisely export our skills in science-technology so that other nations can build up pools of talent of their own. At the same time we should at home do far more than at present to make certain science-technology is used not merely to produce new goods at random but to achieve a better society through improved education, nutrition and medical care—in short, an ever-expanding human environment.

Recently I read in the Paris newspaper *Le Monde* a rather plaintive query that translates roughly as: "Why is it that man has been able to produce explosives on the scale of 25 pounds of TNT for every human being, but still has been unable to provide for everyone 25 pounds of rice or grain?" I am convinced that the nation first able to aid the world in producing 25 pounds of rice or grain for every man will find itself a far greater world power than the nation that adds another 25 pounds of TNT per person to the already overly large world stockpile of destruction.

Ideas The third ingredient of a nation's strategy is the effective power of a nation's ideas. By the power of its ideas I mean not only the thinking and production of a nation's philosophers, poets, artists and statesmen, but also the success with which the society realizes for everyone the values in which it claims to believe. We say we stand for freedom, law, orderly change, equality under God; and I believe we do. But the denial of equal rights and opportunities to one section of our people, the riots in our cities, the ever-spreading urban blight, our high level of unemployment and poverty and our strategic bombing of North Vietnam are at least as much a part of our national image as our ideas.

Perhaps we can see our situation in better perspective if we consider how the prestige and power of Communist China have been affected by the recent purges and actions of the Red Guards. The Red Chinese claim to be the wave of the future; they continually proclaim to the new nations of the world that they are the society best organized for orderly progress from underdevelopment to national greatness. Their mastery of the process of nuclear fission greatly added to their power. Chinese, as distinct from Russian, Communism was becoming a growing force in Latin America and also in certain sections of Africa. But the purges and excesses of Mao, the antics of the Red Guards and the dislocation of the economic and intellectual life of the nation have decreased Chinese influence. Nations formerly aligned with China, such as Indonesia, have broken away. The obvious gap between claim and reality has greatly diminished Red China as an international power.

Only the self-deluding can deny that when we engage in a war or use tactics in a war about which most of our allies have grave doubts, or when large sections of our society are on public view as not benefiting from our prosperity, our prestige and power throughout the world are lessened in exactly the same way as the excesses of Maoism reduce the prestige of China. It is undeniably true we have the power to turn North Vietnam into "a parking lot," as certain extremists have recently advocated. But far from solving any problem such an action would leave us alone in the world— feared, distrusted, without friends. In short, such an extreme solution is not only morally repugnant; it would gravely diminish rather than increase our national power. To understand modern strategy is to recognize this conclusion as established beyond doubt. I believe further that each escalation by the President of the strategic bombing of North Vietnam actually decreases U.S. power in the world.

The power of ideas, a third facet of national strategy, has gained importance only recently. Before telecommunications, jet travel, radio and television, ideas spread slowly. In the past little was often known about what was actually happening inside a foreign country. But the generation of scientists that developed "The Bomb" also made communication by satellite possible. Demosthenes remarked, "I can control a crowd as far as I can throw a stone and cast my voice." As a result of the scientific revolution we can, as it were, cast stones into global orbit and a man's voice and actions can be projected instantaneously into every corner of the world. With this instant communication from and to all parts of the world the strategic importance of the power of ideas took a quantum jump.

To the extent that we repair our social fabric so that all participate equally, to the extent that we abolish poverty, to the extent that we provide a climate in which artistic and intellectual commitment flourishes, we will have added to the power of ideas in our national strategy. And like scientific knowledge this power is no less immense for being intangible.

Military Power So we come to the final ingredient of American strategy: the military might of our nation. Many still consider armed force to be the sole element of that strategy. I hope I have been persuasive enough in showing this is not so. I do not mean in the confines of this chapter to go into the tactical complexities of military power any more than I have dealt fully with economics, science, or ideas as they relate to strategy. Again my purpose here is to delineate only the broad outlines of the nature of post-Hiroshima military power, which perhaps is more misunderstood than any other aspect of our national strategy.

In my attempt to dispose of the myth that the correct way for a nation to "wage war" is to use against its adversary all the power it possesses, including nuclear weapons, I stressed that both the United States and Russia now have ample nuclear arms to destroy each other—no matter who strikes first. From such a "thermonuclear exchange," to lapse into technical language, the damage would be, to say the least, vast and awesome. There is one chance out of three that the fallout from our attack on Russia would cause well over 70 per cent casualties in countries as far west as Great Britain. Nations downwind to the south, such as India, would suffer even more heavily, while the Russian attack on the United States would contaminate huge areas of Latin America.

Someday, through greed or miscalculation, nuclear weapons may be used. This is why certain forms of arms control are so all-important. To deter an adversary from using nuclear weapons against us it is vitally necessary that we keep in our strategic arsenal the latest and most sophisticated weapons and counter weapons. As much as possible these weapons should be designed so that whatever enemies we may have realize we do not intend to use our weapons to strike first. But we intend to and will respond massively and lethally against any nuclear "Pearl Harbor" upon ourselves.

But, and I reiterate this important point, the very might, accuracy and destructive power of these nuclear weapons make them unsuitable for anything less than total war. Neither we nor our enemies dare to risk an all-out nuclear counter attack by being the first to employ nuclear weapons in areas where a vital national self-interest is not threatened. The Berlin blockade, the Korean War, the Lebanese crisis and the Cuban missile crisis—all of these challenges to America have been met and solved without a nuclear exchange. None but the fanatic can be dissatisfied with an outcome so obviously beneficial to all mankind.

Our strategic nuclear weapons exist to deter nuclear war. As such they are kept ready but sheathed except in the most extreme crises. They are as unsuited to limited war as a tank is to killing a mosquito. We have devoted a great deal of money, scientific skill and military talent to our strategic nuclear force since the explosion over Hiroshima, both in the Air Force and in the Navy, and to some extent (air defense) in the Army. While there are certain areas in which I would shift the emphasis I can state unhesitatingly that our strategic nuclear force is reliable, effective and ready.

LIMITED WAR

Now we turn to an entirely different area: limited war. Beneath the broad umbrella of nuclear power America faces the possibility of many limited challenges. These will range all the way from strident propaganda or economic boycott, through guerrilla war and subversion, to such bruising confrontations as the Cuban missile crisis or Korea. To meet such less-than-total challenges we need a flexible military establishment to wage less-than-total wars. For such a force we have been niggardly in our expenditures, haphazard in our science, and we have frustrated those of military talent who have tried to wrestle with the problem. We still do not have the forces necessary to fight such wars quickly, in precisely defined areas, and at minimum cost in life and treasure.

What is wanted is a force capable of making the punishment fit the crime. Or, in the language of the tactician, applying power adequate to contain the threat. The absence of a truly modern limited-war capability both makes more likely the possibility of general nuclear war. When we cannot fight a war successfully within limits we are pressed to escalate dangerously; and this in turn makes more difficult intelligent debate on such issues as Vietnam.

Another problem is that the concepts and terms involved in the problem of limited war are not generally understood. For example there is much discussion in America about "a bombing pause." This discussion is confused because the general term "bombing" covers a variety of special military situations. There is the strategic bombing of North Vietnam to which, for reasons detailed in the next chapter, I am totally opposed. There is the strategic bombing of South Vietnam about which I have grave moral and military doubts. There is the interdiction bombing of South Vietnam, much of which I believe necessary. Finally, there is tactical bombing and close air support, both of which I consider essential so long as ground combat continues. Enough. I have merely cited one incomplete example to show the complexity of the issue.

Finally, in this discussion of military tactics it is important to refer back to our overall view of strategy and reiterate that there is no dividing line between war and peace. Just because we fight a limited war, other aspects of strategy do not stop. During the Korean war, for example, skilled diplomacy utilizing the power of the ideas for which we then fought rallied to our cause the support of the United Nations. Even neutralist India sent a hospital unit to Korea. This U.N. presence added to our strength far above and beyond mere units of fire power. And now, in contrast, the almost total lack of such support in Vietnam makes it more difficult for us to bring the war to a successful conclusion.

If we have a society that men believe in and if we are doing our utmost to produce the 25 pounds of rice or wheat for each person in the world, then governments under threat of attack, if forced to call on us for military assistance, will do so with confidence. Their people will welcome us, even as we were welcomed during World War II by the occupied countries of Europe and later in Korea. Before we have fired a single shot we will be close to the sucessful outcome of the battle.

The goal of strategy is peace. Not peace at any price —but the peace that comes through mature and thoughtful utilization of our vast power. We must understand modern strategy, the many facets of our power and the myth-shattering complexities of war in the post-Hiroshima age. Then we can continue our domestic growth, conduct our foreign affairs with a reasonable amount of wisdom and help those who voluntarily ask us for economic or technical aid in the solution of their problems. If we continue in ignorance, we shall expend our nation's wealth and men in never-ending conflicts about the globe. Further we will neglect what must be done at home to achieve within our own society its full potential. And we will reap the wrath and anger of both those we have neglected at home and those we incorrectly believe we aid abroad.

Having considered in this all too brief detail the changed nature of modern strategy and war, let us now turn to Vietnam.

III

VIETNAM: HISTORY
AND RESOLUTION

Vietnam is the least understood conflict in our nation's history. America has committed over 460,000 troops and the might of our air and sea power. We have fought skillfully and bravely. Yet "victory" is nowhere in sight. Will more troops bring a quicker victory? Do we need more air strikes? These are questions that all Americans ask. Our course of action would be simple if the answer were an easy Yes. But unfortunately there will be no "victory" in Vietnam. Only more victims. This is the difficult and unfortunate truth we have yet to understand. To see the Vietnam problem we must first trace briefly the history of our involvement there and then set Vietnam in the context of our present military and diplomatic capabilities. When we have done that, while we may not gain "victory" through a clearer view of the situation we can at least plan toward a successful conclusion of the war.

Before beginning this study of the Vietnamese situation, I want to make one point absolutely clear. On the level of combat on the battlefield Vietnam is the best-fought war in our history. Thanks to a substantial base of experienced training personnel in the United States, our young men enter the combat zone more battle-ready than in previous wars. Morale is helped by the fact that ground combat troops are returned to the United States after a specific number of days in Vietnam. Unlike their predecessors in World War II, they know they will not have to stay in combat until they are killed or wounded—or until the war is brought to an end. I have watched officers and non-coms leading the troops in the field and they are highly professional. Americans, whatever they think of the conflict, can be proud of these soldiers and their dedication to the task at hand. Under the most difficult and dangerous circumstances these soldiers have proved that they are every bit as brave, patriotic, and hard working as their forefathers in uniform. Being of the beatnik or hippie generation has not diminished their qualities as Americans; rather, I am inclined to think, it has added to them. Let no debate on Vietnam divide us from the knowledge of our soldiers' courage. The errors of this tragic war are made, not on the battlefield, but in Washington.

My own involvement with Vietnam began in 1954. I was then Chief of Plans of the Army, serving under Matthew B. Ridgway, the Chief of Staff. I knew Ridgway and had served with him in the past. He is a man of incisive intelligence and great moral courage—in brief, a good man to work for.

At that time in 1954 the French were involved in the defense of Dien Bien Phu. They had chosen to defend this isolated fortified area in an effort to provoke the Vietminh into a major battle in which the Communist troops could be destroyed. But it was clear by then that the battle was not going as the French planned; and they were making tremendous demands on the United States for war material. Vietnam was already becoming a swamp-ridden jungle Moloch with an insatiable appetite for aircraft, arms, ammunition and other military supplies.

The Joint Chiefs of Staff had been doubtful about the Dien Bien Phu strategy from the beginning. Our military adviser in Saigon, Major General Thomas Trapnell, had never thought well of the scheme. I myself had felt that genuine French concessions to make Vietnam independent was far more important in the situation than mere fire power.

As the situation at Dien Bien Phu worsened, the French in desperation asked us for carrier strikes against the Communists attacking the fortified area. Admiral Arthur W. Radford, a strong advocate of carrier air power, then chairman of the Joint Chiefs of Staff, was in favor of such a U.S. military action. So were Chief of Staff of the Air Force Nathan F. Twining and Chief of Naval Operations Robert B. Carney. There was even talk of using one or two nuclear weapons. Secretary of State John Foster Dulles sounded out our allies on their reaction to such a U.S. air attack. Fortunately

General Ridgway refused to bend in his opposition to this "quickie" solution. He believed that the air attacks would be indecisive and further that they would lead to American ground troops being involved in Indochina. We in the Army felt that to fight on the ground in Indochina alongside the French was a war America did not want.

Though under tremendous pressure to conform, Ridgway refused to endorse the majority view. Instead he carried his disagreement over the air strike, or "split" as it is known in Pentagonese, up to the President. I am convinced that Ridgway's determined opposition plus that of our allies was crucial in aborting this early effort to involve us in Vietnam. I well remember my feeling of relief when President Eisenhower's decision went against the strike. A feeling that was regrettably brief.

The situation at Dien Bien Phu worsened and on May 7th it fell. The next day the French sat down in Geneva at the conference table with delegates from Vietnam, the Vietminh regime and six other countries and submitted armistice proposals. Surprisingly quickly, or so it seemed to us in the Pentagon, an agreement was reached to end the then Vietnamese war. The Geneva agreements and Final Declaration of July 1954 provided for Vietnam to be partitioned along the seventeenth parallel into North and South Vietnam, with nationwide elections to determine the nature of reunification to be held in July, 1956. An international control commission was also established to supervise the implementation of the agreements.

To understand what happened next, it is important

to understand the attitude of the Pentagon back in 1954 because this atmosphere led to the initial decisions that brought us to our present position in Vietnam today. And this attitude is still all too prevalent in our military thinking. Indeed it has deep roots elsewhere.

In 1954 the recent Korean War decisively influenced Pentagon thinking. For the Air Force, Korea had been a disillusioning and frustrating experience. Air Force leaders had assumed that air superiority, air surveillance and air attacks would smash the North Korean drive and demolish the North Korean military establishment. They had trumpeted this point of view both to the public and to the President. When the bombing failed to halt the North Korean war effort they developed the myth of the Yalu sanctuary. If only they could bomb Red Chinese Manchuria, which lay beyond the Yalu River, they said, everything would turn out all right. Thus the Air Force was able to avoid, at least in public, confronting the evidence that in Korea both strategically and tactically air power had failed. Unfortunately from their frustration sprang a readiness to answer any challenge to American power with threats of total nuclear war.

To the Army, Korea had been embittering and costly. Of the 147,000 casualties most had been in the ground forces. Despite the Army's wealth of combat experience from World War II, its abundance of logistical support, and its modern fighting equipment, major units had been surprised and routed by Chinese forces. The Army felt that ground forces had done the major share of the fighting, that more wars like the Korean War were a possibility, that the Army's accomplishments should be recognized, and that it should receive the funds to train and equip itself for such contests in the future. Instead the Army was beginning to feel the pressure of the "new look" cutbacks that followed the promulgation of the doctrine of massive retaliation; its funds and troop strengths were slashed while the forces for strategic nuclear bombing were built up.

But above and beyond this, everyone in the Pentagon—including, let me add, myself—tended to see the world in terms of good guys and bad guys. Moreover I met no one who doubted who the good guys were. (It was a simple vision of the world, which held much truth in the period when we faced the byzantine greed of Stalinism.) And we had many supporters outside the Pentagon. Speaking of the Geneva accords in August of 1954, Francis Cardinal Spellman of New York stated:

If Geneva and what was agreed upon there means anything at all, it means . . . taps for the buried hopes of freedom in Southeast Asia. . . . Now the devilish techniques of brainwashing, forced confessions and rigged trials have a new locale for their exercise. . . . Communism has a world plan and it has been following a carefully set-up timetable for the achievement of that plan. . . .

We had excuses for our belief. Still, we should have been wiser.

Instead we assumed that Peking was a mere pawn of Moscow, that thwarted by NATO (North Atlantic Treaty Organization) and the Marshall Plan from taking over Europe, Stalin was now on the march in Asia. The

Communist world was assumed to be an integrated, monolithic bloc. Only a few of us were beginning to distinguish between the nationalistic Communism of Tito and the Stalinism of Russia; I can recall the hours of thought I devoted to the question before recommending the Army's support of military aid to Tito. And for even fewer of us did that clearer vision extend as far as the Vietnamese brand of Communism under Ho Chi Minh. The belief that Communism itself was changing and that there were types of nationalistic Communism with which the United States could quite safely coexist would have been regarded as close to heresy.

It was in this atmosphere that we closely followed the negotiations at Geneva. We had the feeling that the French had not only failed in combat, but that now they were about to let down the team. Despite our lavish support of their efforts to reestablish themselves in Indochina, they were now acting in their own self-interest, rather than in the interest of the free world as a whole. Through intelligence sources we learned about what later became known as the Sainteny Commission, named for its chairman, whose purpose was to negotiate directly with the Ho Chi Minh government to assure the safety of French investments in Communist-held territory.

Parenthetically, I had occasion some years later, in December 1965, to discuss at lunch the Sainteny Commission with General de Gaulle. General Paul Ely, who had been the French commander in Vietnam in late 1954, was also present. I asked General de Gaulle how the commission got along with Ho Chi Minh; he assured me that they had worked well together. When I asked him whether he thought a similar modus vivendi could be made with whatever type of government appeared in Saigon in the event North and South Vietnam settled their differences, he said without hesitation that he was confident this could be done. It is important to remember these remarks when evaluating French pronouncements on Vietnam and to be aware that France was concerned about protecting a rather large economic investment.

But to return to 1954, the attitude of the Pentagon staff when the Geneva accords were finally reached was that the French had unwisely folded. Now it was obviously up to us to assume the full burden of combat against Communism in that area. Secretary of State John Foster Dulles and the Central Intelligence Agency (CIA) agreed with the Pentagon. At that time Secretary Dulles was building, as a good lawyer might, a paper wall of treaties to contain Communism. Germany joined NATO, then came SEATO (Southeast Asia Treaty Organization), and then CENTO (Central Treaty Organization). In this atmosphere the Joint Chiefs began with the highest priority to study a proposal to send combat troops into the Red River delta of North Vietnam.

As Chief of Plans of the Army Staff I was responsible for recommending what attitude the Army should take toward this proposal to put American ground troops into North Vietnam. I began by bringing together the best Asian experts. We decided that to be honest with ourselves we had to face the fact that if we entered North Vietnam we were going to war, not with Ho Chi Minh, but with Red China. Red China would be providing most of the arms, vehicles, ammunition, and other sinews of war because of what she would feel was a threat to her national self-interest. Once again, let me reiterate that this did not mean that either I or the Army staff wanted or urged war with Red China. In the weeks and months to come we were to argue forcefully and frequently against such a war. Rational consideration of the alternatives should not be mistaken for advocacy.

Having assumed Red China as the enemy, we had to further assume that the entry of an expeditionary force into the Hanoi area would bring a reaction from the Chinese, exactly as they had reacted when we crossed the 38th Parallel in Korea. If this happened we would find ourselves confronting Chinese field armies that vastly outnumbered our own forces. And we would not have the narrow peninsula in which they could be contained as in Korea. We were also in agreement that we had to prepare for the reopening of the Korean front by the Chinese if we committed ourselves heavily to Vietnam. Then followed the agonizing decision as to whether we should wait to be attacked in Korea, or whether we should take the initiative in reopening that front.

Remembering our experience in World War II and Korea, the Army staff anticipated a bloody and costly war that would engage a tremendous portion of our manpower and national wealth. This cost could be met only at the expense of our other global commitments and by the diversion of resources from the well-being of our domestic society. In all probability we would have to resort to tax increases, wage controls and rationing.

As to Vietnam itself, we put the size of the necessary expeditionary force at eight combat divisions, supported by thirty-five engineer battalions, and all the artillery and logistical support such mammoth undertakings require. (At the time of my trip to Vietnam in November 1967 there were eight and two-thirds U.S. divisions in Vietnam.) Because of the size of the undertaking and the danger of involvement with Red China, we believed it would be necessary to call up the Army Reserves and National Guard. In short, we felt the operation should not be attempted unless the country was put on virtually a war footing.

Again, as at the time of Dien Bien Phu the Joint Chiefs divided. Admiral Radford was emphatically in favor of landing a force in the Haiphong-Hanoi area, even if it meant risking war with Red China. In this he was fully supported by the Chief of Staff of the Air Force and the Chief of Naval Operations. In my opinion such an operation meant a great risk of war. Just southeast of Haiphong harbor is the island of Hainan, which is part of Red China. The Navy was unwilling to risk their ships in the Haiphong area without first invading and capturing the island. Admiral Radford and the Chiefs of the Navy and Air Force felt that, faced with our overwhelming power, the Red Chinese would not react to this violation of their sovereignty. General Ridgway and I had grave doubts about the validity of this reasoning.

Once more the embattled Ridgway "split." Using the staff study we had prepared in the Army he wrote directly to President Eisenhower, pointing out the hazards to the nation if we undertook such a war in Vietnam and the dubious gains. Again fortunately, the President decided not to commit U.S. forces to Southeast Asia.

However, there was a compromise. We would not attack North Vietnam, but we would support a South Vietnamese government that we hoped would provide a stable, independent government that was representative of the people. As I said before, we saw ourselves as the good guys. The French had let us down, but we would continue the battle. Also, we in the Army were so relieved that we had blocked the decision to commit ground troops to Vietnam that we were in no mood to quibble over the compromise.

Early in 1955 I visited Saigon to discuss political and economic problems plus military aid and assistance with General Paul Ely, chief of the French mission, and Lieutenant General John "Iron Mike" O'Daniel, head of the American mission. At that time I met Ngo Dinh Diem, the prime minister.

Diem seemed to me to be a nonpolitical man, self-centered and quite unresponsive to the needs of his people. However, in October of that year Diem polled 98 per cent of the vote against Emperor Bao Dai. Three days after this referendum Diem proclaimed South Vietnam a republic and himself president. The Department of Defense, the Department of State and the CIA undertook to support him. This involvement in Vietnam sprang from our honest conviction once again that the world was either black or white with no gray in-between. We had stopped Communism in Europe. We had stopped it in Korea. Now we were going to stop it on the seventeenth parallel of Indochina. Unfortunately even today there seems to be some in government who continue to hold this simplistic view, refusing to adjust it to the real world.

Once again the knowledge gap weakens us.

Earlier, on July 16, 1955, while Diem was still premier only, his government had announced with American backing that it would not comply with the Final Declaration of the Geneva Conference that called for free elections to determine the future of all Vietnam. The reason given was that free choice was impossible in the North. In acquiescing in the Diem announcement, the United States violated its own unilateral declaration giving its position on the Geneva Conference, which stated that the United States "shall continue to seek to achieve unity through free elections supervised by the U.N., to insure that they are conducted fairly. . . . The United States reiterates its traditional position that peoples are entitled to determine their own future. . . ."

At the time of Diem's declaration the number of French troops in South Vietnam was still significant. But by October when Premier Diem deposed the absentee Emperor Bao Dai and became the first president of the Republic of South Vietnam the French presence had begun to disappear rapidly. President Eisenhower sent President Diem a letter in which he offered U.S. assistance "in maintaining a strong, viable state, capable of resisting attempted subversion or aggression through military means. . . ." Later President Eisenhower explained that this language was meant to cover aid only. And during the Eisenhower administration the U.S. Military Assistance Advisory Group, averaging six hundred and fifty men, did not increase significantly.

President Kennedy began to occupy himself with the

Southeast Asian situation immediately after his inauguration. By then the resistance movement in South Vietnam,
the Vietcong and its political arm, the National Front
for the Liberation of South Vietnam (NLF), had gained
strength. The NLF was receiving some aid and direction from the Vietminh in the North. The degree and
extent of this aid and control have been from the beginning the subject of bitter debate within the U.S. government; the scarcity of facts has not dampened the heat of
the argument.

With President Kennedy's election I returned to government service as ambassador to France. I called on the
President on May 18, 1961 to discuss his planned visit
to Paris. The talk soon shifted to Southeast Asia, particularly Vietnam and Laos. At that time Laos appeared
the more volatile situation of the two. I argued strongly
against committing any U.S. troops to Laos. I pointed
out that Laos was a landlocked area in which it would
be very difficult to bring U.S. power to bear in any
meaningful way, even if it should be in the U.S. interest
to do so. I felt Laos would turn into a bottomless pit into
which we would pour soldier after soldier. I recounted
for the President the history of the debate inside the
Pentagon after Dien Bien Phu and said I felt this new
situation was similar. There was little to be gained and
a great deal to be risked by U.S. military action.

In the discussion President Kennedy indicated strongly
that he believed sending U.S. troops to Laos was the
wrong course of action. He also implied that if he asked
the Pentagon for advice they would recommend dispatch-

ing troops. I agreed with him—I thought a significant number of generals and admirals still lived in the "good and bad guys" world.

The President suggested that I call on Prince Souvanna Phouma of Laos in Paris and try to persuade him that the American objective was truly "to establish a free, neutral, independent Laos." Up to this point the United States had been backing the CIA-picked General Phoumi Nosavan; and the President wanted to make it clear our policy had shifted to the support of Souvanna Phouma.

There was a good deal of suspicion of Souvanna Phouma in the U.S. government. It was felt he was, if not a Communist himself, pretty much controlled by the Communists. But the President argued, and hindsight convinces me more than ever he was completely correct, that Souvanna Phouma was the man the Laotians wanted and that he should receive U.S. support. My job was to convince Souvanna Phouma of our intention to respect the freedom, neutrality and independence of Laos.

Shortly after President Kennedy's visit to Paris I called on Souvanna Phouma at his Paris apartment. His attitude was not entirely friendly toward me, but he seemed willing to listen. Among other things I tried to persuade him to visit the United States, meet President Kennedy and learn firsthand of the United States change in attitude. Souvanna Phouma seemed loath to do this, though he had a trip planned for the immediate future that would take him through several Communist countries. I was not sure I had accomplished much at the meeting.

I called on him again about a month later and this time felt that genuine progress was made. Souvanna Phouma was quite friendly and we got along well. I continued to visit with him frequently after that and reassure him of the genuineness of American intentions. In the end I am satisfied he became convinced of our sincerity. Finally, through the ability and craft of W. Averell Harriman in Geneva, a treaty was drafted which was acceptable to all parties. Once again the commitment of U.S. troops to Southeast Asia had been avoided.

While Laos then is not Vietnam now, there are distinct parallels. The Laotian experience convinced me of the need to work in Asia with national leaders of differing political persuasion, as we had with Tito in Yugoslavia. That we cannot remake the world in our own image is a truism often repeated but not always followed. And have we looked at our own image recently? Laos also convinced me of the fallacy of the falling-domino theory. Laos went neutral; neither Cambodia nor Thailand fell. With a little diplomatic skill dominoes can be buttressed; it sometimes seems to me that we deliberately try to link them to each other.

In the meantime in Vietnam things were not going well with the Diem government, though we were doing our verbal best to help him. Vice-President Johnson had visited the country in 1961 and referred to Diem as the "Churchill of Asia." Shortly thereafter Secretary of Defense Robert S. McNamara, on one of his frequent brief tours of inspection, called Diem "one of the greatest leaders of our time." Yet the Diem government became more isolated and oppressive. By 1963 the war in Vietnam was going very badly and President Kennedy was having grave doubts about our course of action. Recent books have indicated the depth and bitterness of the division in the Kennedy administration over Vietnam.

The President himself stated publicly at that time, "In the final analysis it is their war. They are the ones that have to win it or lose it. We can help them, give them equipment. We can send our men out there as advisers. But they have to win it."

However, the President's military advisers continued to tell him the war was going well. On October 2, 1963, after another whirlwind visit to Vietnam, Secretary McNamara insisted that the President issue the following statement:

> The military program in South Vietnam has made progress and is sound in principle, though improvements are being energetically sought. . . . Secretary McNamara and General Taylor reported their judgment that the major part of the U.S. military task can be completed by the end of 1965. . . . They reported that by the end of this year [1963] the U.S. program for training Vietnamese should have progressed to the point that one thousand U.S. military personnel assigned to South Vietnam can be withdrawn.

A President deserves better counsel than this from his military advisers!

There has been much speculation about what President Kennedy would or would not have done in Vietnam had he lived. Having discussed military affairs with him often and in detail for fifteen years, I know he was totally opposed to the introduction of combat troops in Southeast Asia. His public statements just before his murder support this view. That the evil that men do should so often live after them while the good is interred with their bones is tragedy enough. Let us not also lay blame on the dead for our own failures.

By 1964 Vietnam had become a major political issue in the presidential campaign. President Johnson reassured those whom he was later to refer to as "nervous Nellies" with the words "I have not chosen to enlarge the war." He later reiterated, "We aren't going to send American boys nine thousand or ten thousand miles away to do what the Asian boys ought to be doing for themselves."

In August 1964, under circumstances still not totally clear, two U.S. destroyers were attacked by North Vietnamese PT boats. President Johnson ordered "air action" against "gunboats and certain supporting facilities" in North Vietnam. In the excitement following the attack on the destroyers, Congress, at the behest of the administration, adopted the Southeast Asia Resolution upon which the administration bases its action today. On February 7, 1965, the first air strikes were ordered against North Vietnam. On March 6 two U.S. marine battalions were landed in South Vietnam. The direct U.S. involvement in Southeast Asia, against which some of us had fought for so long, had begun in earnest. By October 1965 draft calls were the largest since the Korean War and American forces in South Vietnam totaled 148,300.

At this time, though now out of government, I once again felt a grave personal concern for the future. My concern was on two distinct levels. First I was distressed that so much of our physical wealth and human energy should be diverted from our urgent domestic problems. Even back then the war in Vietnam was costing more each day than the entire budget of the domestic peace corps. Secondly, I was convinced from my personal knowledge and expertise that as a military operation Vietnam made no sense.

Bombing was not going to bring Ho Chi Minh to his knees. The strategic bombing survey undertaken by the Air Force after World War II showed that German production had actually risen throughout the Allied bombing effort against Nazi Germany. And even in devastated towns such as Hamburg the morale of the Germans had remained high. More important for the Vietnamese situation were lessons from the recent successful British war against the Communist guerrillas in Malaya. There the British high command made exactly the opposite decision from ours. They began by bombing the areas of suspected guerrilla strength but later halted the bombing campaign because they discovered that the indiscriminate brutality of the bombing aroused the ill will of the people and increased the strength of the guerrilla forces.

Since bombing would not bring Ho to the conference table, it followed that if we were to have our "victory" we would have to commit an ever-growing number of ground troops to the war. There are definite contributions that sophisticatedly handled ground troops can make in a guerrilla war. But unless the people of the country prefer the government supported by foreign troops to the guerrillas (as was the situation in South Korea), the mere introduction of large numbers of ground troops with modern equipment will not resolve the military conflict.

Since the government in Saigon did not appear to have

the necessary people's support, I believed the war would not go well and consequently the Pentagon and certain sections of Congress would call for more troops and heavier bombing until through escalation we confronted directly the power of Red China. This in turn could lead directly to a nuclear World War III. It may be that if China continues to develop nuclear weapons and at the same time pursues her present course she will eventually bring on herself and therefore on the world a nuclear war. But certainly that time is not yet here.

Knowing the history of our Vietnamese involvement, being familiar with the country and gravely concerned for the future, I tried in my own mind to apply my knowledge of diplomacy and warfare to developing some strategy to bring the war to a successful conclusion. I evolved what has come to be known as the "enclave" strategy. I tried in various ways to advance this strategy as a possible alternative to our gradual escalation of the war and immediately found myself in the middle of what can mildly be described as violent controversy.

I believe the enclave strategy to be even more valid today than it was in 1965. Combined with a halt in the bombing of North Vietnam it constitutes a vital first step in our de-escalation of the war. My reasoning behind the enclave strategy is as follows.

As discussed in the previous chapter, the primary tactical problem once a war occurs is to keep it limited. This is particularly true of a war in which we should not have become involved where the interests of the United States were at best marginal. Therefore I looked for a way of halting the buildup while successfully holding what we had and opening negotiations with the Vietcong and Vietminh.

I remembered from my own experience that the key to Italy had been the capture and development of the port and airfields around Naples. Later, control of the port and airfield complex around Cherbourg enabled us to break out of Normandy and carry the battle across France. And in the later stages of the war the port of Antwerp was essential to the main effort in northern Europe in the winter of 1944 and the spring of 1945.

By the fall of 1965 the United States had built up enclaves in Vietnam such as the vast logistical facilities at Camranh Bay, Danang, and Saigon. I believed we should stop the ever-increasing flow of troops, hold the enclaves that we had, and encourage as much as we could a democratic South Vietnamese government in these areas. We would assist the South Vietnamese in bringing their own troops up to a high standard of combat performance. At the same time, it was important to actively search for a diplomatic solution to the war, while using our secure hold on the enclaves as a decisive bargaining counter.

Those were the military and diplomatic tactics that I advocated at that time in 1965, when the United States forces in Vietnam numbered a quarter of a million men. Today we have roughly double that number. Therefore, adoption of a program that places primary emphasis on such enclaves could lead to an immediate reduction in the number of United States troops engaged in the Vietnamese conflict. (Ironically, U.S. forces in Vietnam are now using parts of the enclave strategy, but we need to go further.)

I fully realize the problems of negotiating with the NLF and the government of North Vietnam. They are a tough, determined foe. For over twenty years they have been at war with the Japanese, with European colonists and with the Americans. Our knowledge of them is distorted by distance, our own propaganda, and the antics of some of their "friends." However, indications of the true situation have been given by such impartial observers as Harrison Salisbury of the *New York Times* and the highly respected David Schoenbrun, both of whom have visited North Vietnam. Their reports substantiate those of other observers that say the bombing, far from destroying the morale of that country, has unified the people and increased their determination to fight. As Schoenbrun wrote:

> Anyone who drives down Mandarin Road, as this correspondent did, learns how cruelly futile American bombing has been, for it has only wrought physical destruction and failed utterly to accomplish any military or psychological purpose.
> It has filled people with hatred and redoubled their determination to fight on harder than ever.

There has been nothing written by any observer on the scene that disagrees with this. The only disagreement would seem to be in Washington, where the administration, the generals, and certain senators still reject the evidence of Malaya, Korea and World War II and insist that each escalation of air power will bring Ho Chi Minh one step closer to the negotiating table.

One argument in favor of the bombing that seems to me particularly specious is that to halt the bombing while continuing the ground war against guerrillas would be to "play the enemy's game"—when by striking at him from the air we force North Vietnam to "play our game." Our objective in Vietnam has been to defend the Saigon government on the grounds that the Vietnamese people prefer it to Vietminh or Vietcong rule. The Communists are determined to prove the contrary. That is "the game" both we and the Communists committed ourselves to play. How is this game influenced by bombing North Vietnam? Or for that matter, by the strategic bombing of South Vietnam?

If I had told you I could beat you at a game of chess, and you had challenged me to a game, and halfway through, as I was obviously losing, I kicked over the board and said, "See, I beat you." Might not more than my ability as a chess player be suspect?

The Hanoi government has stated its position officially on several occasions. Probably the most significant of the statements is the four points laid down by Premier Pham Van Dong on April 13, 1965.

1. According to the Geneva Agreement, the United States must withdraw from South Vietnam United States troops, military bases, etc.
2. Pending the peaceful reunification of Vietnam, the provisions of the 1954 Geneva Agreement pertaining to no military alliances, foreign bases, etc., must be respected.

3. The internal affairs of South Vietnam must be settled in accordance with the program of the NLF.

4. The peaceful reunification of Vietnam is to be settled by the Vietnamese people in both zones, without any foreign interference.

The North Vietnamese government has indicated on several occasions in the past that these points were a basis for talks rather than a precondition to them. While the attitude of the Communists does seem to have stiffened with the intensified bombing, Radio Hanoi has indicated several times in 1967 that it is ready to "examine and study" proposals for negotiations if only the bombing be brought to a halt: "definitely and unconditionally."

Meanwhile the war assumes a definitely Orwellian character. Images of violence and blood flash into our living rooms on TV screens. The goals and principles for which we began the conflict lie close to forgotten. Brave men die. In Vietnam experts told me privately the war could last five to ten more years. Yet both sides seem to lack the will or the ability to extricate themselves from the nightmare.

We seem to have forgotten that one of the vital aspects of a limited war is that it be limited in time. A war may involve a minor portion of the total resources of a nation and may be limited to a small area, but if it goes on for four or five years at a reasonably intense level, it is not truly a limited war.

To fight over a village once may result in the deaths of some civilians. Such deaths are always to be regretted, but in both World War II and Korea we killed civilians.

[61]

But if the village is fought over five or six times a great many civilians will die. The whole pattern of life in the village will be altered. If our objective was a better life for the people in that village, as the war continues to drag on we ourselves destroy the objective for which we fight. Destruction is a function of time as well as of weapons and area.

This is a complex thought but an important one. We all know the difference between touching a hot stove for half a second or a few seconds. In Korea we gained our initial objective, the expulsion of the North Koreans from South Korea, in a reasonably short period of time. The war began on June 25, 1960; by October 25 of the same year, four months later, not only had South Korea been cleared of the enemy, but the capital of North Korea had also been seized. Thereafter, the advance to the Yalu and the intervention of the Chinese Communists created a different story. But even then the fighting was mostly on the soil of North Korea. We were not destroying the fabric of social life in South Korea, the land we had come to protect.

We settled the Laotian situation on the basis of a "free, neutral and independent" Laos. A solution of this type should be acceptable in Vietnam. Such a government, tied neither to China, the Soviet Union, nor the West, would be in the best interests of both the Vietnamese people and ourselves. I personally do not believe that Ho Chi Minh ever wanted to be a Chinese puppet or a Chinese satellite. Nor does he wish to be a Russian one. The information we have indicates he is a patriot, an intense nationalist, albeit a Communist—a man who

[62]

tends toward the combination of nationalism and Communism associated with Marshal Tito.

But every day the war continues at its present level peace becomes more difficult to achieve. For we force Ho Chi Minh to depend in ever-increasing extent on Red China for supplies and moral support. From this dependency follows Red Chinese control. We also drive Ho Chi Minh toward Moscow and again he loses his freedom of action. We should be aware that though the Soviet Union professes to wish for a peace settlement, Russia gains several short-term advantages from our involvement in Vietnam. We waste our treasure and our energy; our attention is occupied while she moves in more important areas (as in the Middle East); and finally, we keep the malevolence of Red China directed at us rather than her.

Turning to South Vietnam, here the continuation of the war forces the NLF into dependency upon Hanoi. Not only does this adversely affect the prospect for peace; but it makes independent action for the NLF more difficult after the close of hostilities. Thus in part our military action tends to create the very Communist monolith we entered the war to avoid.

So we force the NLF to dependency on Hanoi, Hanoi into the arms of Peking, and help all three to unite with Russia. Is this wise? Surely a better strategy for America would be to reduce our commitment in Vietnam as promptly as we reasonably can and to turn our energies to realizing the full potential of our society.

I am certain the achievement of peace will be difficult. To succeed we must take extraordinary diplomatic steps to secure fruitful negotiations. The President should appoint, with the advice of the Senate, a special Cabinet-level official of national and international stature to negotiate with the NLF and Hanoi. The sole responsibility of this official would be the termination of the Vietnamese war. He would be served by his own staff and be free from bureaucratic interference and the burden of past positions. In the chaos following World War II we appointed such an individual and gave him the necessary powers when we created the Marshall Plan. The time is graver now. With a reasoned military strategy and the full energies of our government devoted to diplomacy, I am convinced the Vietcong and Vietminh will come to the negotiating table.

The following steps should be taken promptly.

1) All bombing of North Vietnam should be stopped immediately, not just because the Communists want it stopped, but because strategic bombing of the north is counter-productive. In a bombing termination, strategy and morality coincide.

2) Extraordinary and energetic measures should be taken by our government to enter into negotiations with the NLF and the Hanoi government. We have contacted their representatives in the past. These contacts should be reopened. Negotiations should be handled by a specially appointed Cabinet-level official, operating with the full confidence of the President.

3) We should develop and put into operation a plan for the de-escalation of our forces. This plan should be based on the enclave strategy previously discussed.

I anticipate an elated reaction in the United States to the first moves toward peace in Vietnam, for by now people realize that we are on an unwise course. To continue the war is not a test of our national stamina, or of our endurance, or of our courage—as Communist propaganda trumpets to the world. For we know, and Hanoi and Peking know, that if we wanted to lay waste all Vietnam, our nuclear weapons could do so all too easily. What is at test is our wisdom, our common sense. Do we wish by our own actions to bring nuclear war closer on the issue of Vietnam?

Despite the daily increase in the understanding of the Vietnamese problem throughout the country, I would anticipate bitter criticism of any plan that ultimately involves a United States phase-out from Vietnam. Harsh words will come from Congressional leaders who have advocated increased bombing. Some in the veterans' organizations and portions of the professional military establishment will find it difficult to accept a solution that to them appears to be not "victory" but appeasement. At the same time, extremists of the far left will decry as "imperialism" any safeguards necessary for ourselves and the South Vietnamese who have been our friends.

These divisive forces that may well form will put more strain on our already taut social fabric. But wise leadership should be able to anticipate and forestall much of the bitterness and rancor, even though negotiations once under way may well stretch out over a long period of time. When our purpose is achieved, we will have gained less than "victory." But we will have suffered far less than "defeat."

The French experience in ending the Algerian war

should be instructive to us. Many thought that war could not be negotiated to a successful conclusion. Yet, through concerted and flexible diplomacy, plus a firm but restrained military posture, peace came to Algeria. Those Frenchmen who remained behind were not massacred. And for some years France retained enclaves of power that had been an important bargaining counter in the final settlement.

Reaching a settlement will be emotionally difficult and time-consuming; it will tax our wisdom and patience. But our own self-interest makes a settlement imperative. It cannot be repeated too often that its alternative is continued escalation until we confront the forces of Red China in World War III.

Those who advocate escalating the war in Vietnam to the bitter end should realize that their strategy places the United States in a strange position. During the Cuban missile crisis, Khrushchev showed himself willing and able to withdraw from a commitment when resolute action by the United States demonstrated he had over-extended himself in an area outside his basic strategic interest. He tried to place missiles in Cuba; the situation turned against him; he withdrew. It seems to me that those who urge the United States to sharply increase its power in Vietnam demonstrate that the Soviets are more flexible in their foreign policy than we are. Premier Khrushchev was able to overrule those of his advisers who insisted on taking the risk of nuclear war over Cuba, and adjust to his mistakes without great loss of Russian prestige. Do those who advocate continued escalation really believe we are not strong or great enough to do the same?

I began the history of our involvement in Vietnam by saying that at the start of it in 1954 we had seen the world as divided between good and bad guys. This has been the usual way we Americans react. We fought both world wars as if involved in a morality play, with choices clean and clear and actions well defined. Yet victory in those simple terms did not bring the peace we sought.

With Vietnam we are no longer in a morality play. We have grown up into tragedy. We cannot end our involvement there without some cost, some pain. A mature nation can face such realities and take actions which, while less than some want, nevertheless lead outward instead of toward the dark risk of self-destruction. I am sure we can.

IV

WORLD AFFAIRS

Historically, in world affairs the United States has considered itself to be an island in a world of foreigners; hence our dealings with other countries are referred to as our foreign policy. The term "foreign policy" has never seemed totally accurate to me. There is something vaguely offensive and arrogant about it. I would prefer international affairs, or perhaps external affairs. But since foreign policy is accepted usage, I will employ the term.

American foreign policy has seldom been characterized by a sense of initiative. Traditionally, we have always thought of ourselves as a bastion surrounded by foreigners. Our "policies" have never had a conceptual base, a fundamental understanding of what we believe to be our place in world society. We have managed our affairs through improvisation and expediency. Lately, under the pressure of scientific and technological change, our policy appears more and more to be based upon ambiguities and misunderstandings. These are both exceedingly dangerous cornerstones upon which to build a foreign policy structure. We face such results as the Vietnamese war and the slow decay of NATO.

Our foreign policy began with the admonishment of George Washington: "It is our true policy to steer clear of permanent alliances with any portion of the foreign world." Essentially negative in character, this was the precept followed by a young revolutionary nation seeking to detach itself from Europe. It provided the reference point for foreign policy decisions for many years, and indeed it still permeates the thinking of some people. For many years our interest in foreign affairs was limited and, generally speaking, the United States did not actively enter into global affairs in a significant way until World War I. That was a costly experience in terms of manpower and national wealth. At its end we found thrust upon us a role of leadership we were loath to accept. Congress rejected President Wilson's Fourteen Points. And, in the twenties the country slowly slipped back to the good old preoccupation with domestic affairs.

Isolationism was rampant by the mid-1930's. The Kellogg-Briand pact of 1928 had supposedly outlawed war as an instrument of national policy. We were deeply preoccupied with the great depression that began in the fall of 1929 and were unconcerned about events abroad, although the fighting in Ethiopia, about which the League of Nations could do nothing, and the rise of Hitler indicated to some Americans the possibility of hostilities ahead. At the same time the Soviet Union was emerging as a great power, exploiting the economic depression in the United States and menacing small countries around its periphery.

[69]

Hitler's conquests and Pearl Harbor moved the country from isolationism into World War II. Again we spent our manpower and wealth. Again at the end we turned rapidly back to domestic affairs, placing our hopes for future peace on the newly established United Nations. The Soviet Union soon made it clear it did not intend to release the countries it had seized during World War II. The Iron Curtain rang down. With jet aircraft, electronic communications, and nuclear weapons shrinking the world, the United States was forced to search for some other foreign policy than mere avoidance of external problems.

CONTAINMENT

In July of 1947 there appeared in *Foreign Affairs* the famous article signed "X" and called "The Sources of Soviet Conflict." Later *Life* described the article as "causing a sensation because it is believed that it expresses the official U.S. view of why the Russians act as they do." It later turned out that "X" was George F. Kennan, a man of long experience in the foreign service, who knew the Russians well. The article concluded that "the main elements of any United States policy toward the Soviet Union must be that of a long-term, patient but firm and vigilant containment of Russian expansionist tendencies."

From this intellectual beginning sprang the Age of Containment. Upon a policy of containment was built a treaty wall: a series of organizations—NATO, SEATO, and CENTO—designed to contain militant

Communism. Actually, containment was eventually carried much further than the establishment of these treaties, and became a pervasive philosophy penetrating every nook and cranny of foreign policy. The American people were sold on containment. It was simple to understand, and reasonable in its appeal. President Johnson expressed it on his visit to Vietnam in 1967 when he addressed the troops, "They want something we've got and we're not gonna let 'em have it."

I am not sure how much virtue there is in consistency; but I was against containment as an all-inclusive strategic doctrine in 1947, and remain against it today. To me flexibility has always been important. The ability to recognize both opportunity and change, to give and take. It seemed to me that with containment a certain rigidity entered into our foreign policy. We hardened and developed a resistance to change that at the end has led to Vietnam.

Basic to the doctrine of containment was the assumption that the Communist side was, and would remain, an integrated monolithic power bloc controlled by a few ruthless and greedy men. On the Communist side there were certain to be economic constraints, conscription of labor, regimentation of education, and all of the trappings of a totalitarian state. On the non-Communist side would be a happy, growing society, providing institutions for government of each nation's own choosing, an ever-increasing abundance of products, better and better education, and an opportunity for all citizens to go as far and as high as their talents allowed.

On neither side have these assumptions turned out as

anticipated. The Soviets have done well in science, in education, and in medical care, to name but a few areas where significant advances have occurred. In Russia, and to a lesser extent in some other Communist countries, more and more consumer products have become available and the people demand still more. An economy that was entirely production-oriented has creakingly and ponderously turned toward a market orientation. The profit motive and the principle of incentive and reward are becoming increasingly important. At the same time the military establishment has grown sizable and modern. Rocket rattling characterizes the May Day parades rather than the achievements of labor.

But even with such improvements the deadening effect of a totalitarian society still caused many, including Stalin's daughter, Svetlana Alliluyeva, to defect. In 1956, uprisings in Hungary and Warsaw revealed gross inadequacies in the life behind the Iron Curtain.

More importantly, nationalism has proven to be stronger than Communism. Yugoslavia, Red China and Albania, for example, have all made clear their independence of Moscow's Communism. As these and other former satellites have increased in stature they have grown more and more restive. National independence and identification with their own history and aspirations become the rallying cry.

Conditions in the United States I describe in detail elsewhere. Here we should note that while we live in an affluent economy where we buy more and more things and where our productivity grows at an astonishing rate, we have become increasingly poor in our spiritual and cultural values. And while many enjoy increased abundance, there are still millions living at a substandard level. Equal opportunity for jobs, wealth, housing and education has not been achieved. An estimated twenty million Americans live in poverty. The cost of medical care is rising; we have made scant provision for our old and sick. To an increasing extent each summer brings unprecedented violence to our cities. We have half a million men committed to a major war in Southeast Asia, costing over two billion dollars a month and therefore forcing a cutback in many essential domestic programs.

The rest of the world is changing, much of it seeking ways to cooperate and live together. We, on the other hand, appear to be embarked upon a role of using power for power's sake, a course of action that may bring World War III. We justify this, and the neglect of our domestic condition, by pointing backward at the Communist threat of the early 1950's. The world of 1984, prophesied so vividly by George Orwell, seems to be already with us.

Fear remains a powerful force in the USSR, as in other nations. Foreign offices all too often base policy on fear rather than on aspirations and hope. The time has come for America to lead the way to a change. The world has shrunk too much for men to live in constant fear of each other. The scientific revolution has given man many radically new modes of communication; he should use them to talk to and try to understand his fellow man.

The man in the street today has more information instantly available to him then did a prime minister of a generation ago. This is the Age of Exposure, the age when more and more information is available to more and more people. The average citizen can learn what is going on directly at the very scene of activity, whether it be a police station in Dallas, the battlefield in Vietnam, a political uprising in Latin America or a business conference in Europe.

At the same time many former European colonies in Africa and the Far East have become independent. The relationship among governments is going through as profound a change as any other in this revolutionary period. As Walter Lippmann recently expressed it:

> The international order which evolved since the Middle Ages, the order imposed and managed by the Western great powers, has been shattered. There are some who think we can return to that old order, with the United States replacing the Great Britain of the nineteenth century. But all who think this, President Johnson and Secretary Rusk and Mr. Nixon, for example, merely compound the confusion and anarchy of the international order. It is a naive illusion that 1967 is 1939, that Southeast Asia is Western Europe, that Mao Tse-tung is Hitler and that Lyndon Johnson is Churchill. It is not producing a firm and free international order but the largest quagmire in which this country has ever floundered.

It seems to me that we neglect these words at our peril. If we fully realize our ideals our society will be more responsive to the spiritual and material needs of people than any other system of government. Nations will come to us to choose as models for their own society the parts of our system they wish to duplicate, even as they now borrow from our technocracy. They came to us so in our past. If we live our professed values they will come again. We will be able to meet and surmount any form of totalitarianism, whether of the right or the left, to compete in the marketplace, in the laboratory, at the easel, if forced to on the battlefield, or any other place where the spirit of man is tested.

EUROPE

The area of primary concern to the United States has traditionally been Europe; ethnically, culturally, and economically we are close to it. We have fought two wars there and in recent years, as our outlook has matured, we have begun to enter with Europe into a cohesive political and military union. At the same time Western Europe itself, politically and economically, has been drawing closer together. This new spirit of European cooperation emerged with difficulty because Western Europe has been composed traditionally of small political groups, many of whose origins go back to the dark pages of history. But since World War II Europe, despite the disparate background of its countries, has accomplished miracles of economic and military unity.

The idea of a European union is not a new one. At the corner of one of the most lovely spots in Paris, the Place des Vosges, is a bronze plaque quoting Victor Hugo: "I represent a party which does not yet exist; the party of revolution, civilization. This party will make the twentieth century. There will issue from it first the United States of Europe. . . ." Many years earlier Benjamin Franklin, writing to a banker friend in Paris on October 22, 1787, suggested that they might form "a federal union and one grand republic of all its different states and kingdoms."

Many modern European statesmen have supported the concept of union. General Charles de Gaulle, speaking on the subject on November 14, 1949, said, "I have always believed that the basis for such a Europe was a direct agreement, without intermediaries, between the French people and the German people."

This view, that the integration of Europe must begin with strong partners cooperating together, finds little support in our State Department. For reasons that must stem from our view that in human endeavors biggest is best, we seem to favor a concept of large organizations or alliances. Into these we seek to fit those who we believe qualify for entry. NATO, SEATO and CENTO represent the organization man's approach to solving the essential need for economic, social and military unity.

Observing the recovery of Europe, when the Marshall Plan was carried out, we were a bit hesitant about how far to encourage it. At the time of the Marshall Plan's creation a leading American diplomat described what we wanted as "a Europe so powerful it will stand right up and spit in our eye. We won't like it, but that is what we want." Well, this is what we now have in the European Economic Community (EEC), generally called the European Common Market. Its strength is based upon the strength of its individual members and their willingness to subordinate, to a degree, national need to the common European good. And from our reaction to it not only do we not like it, we have forgotten it was what we wanted.

There is no popularly elected head of the European Economic Community. There is a council of ministers for whom the appointed chairman may speak, but there is no president or prime minister. Their bible is the Treaty of Rome and they intend to abide by it and insist that applicants conform to it. It is important that we in the United States understand this. The United Kingdom, for example, is now seeking entry into the Common Market. Great Britain will be expected to meet all the provisions of the Rome treaty, including those that provide for the free flow of capital and labor, as well as provisions of the agricultural plan. The capital provisions are difficult for the British, since they are partially dependent on U.S. dollar support to hold the pound at its present level.

Here again the Vietnam war poisons that atmosphere. We have insisted on the support of the United Kingdom in Vietnam; in return before devaluation we supported the pound and to a lesser extent continue to do so. Yet both the long-term interest of the United States and the United Kingdom could best be served by British entry into the EEC. By accepting our support for the pound which we pushed on them, the United Kingdom has minimized its chances of entry into the community of Europe. Again we are taking satisfaction from short-term gains while overlooking the long-term necessities of a sound foreign policy.

There are other obstacles to British entry into the EEC. The favored economic position that the commonwealth nations now have with Great Britain would have to be negotiated. A period of long and difficult transition lies ahead. But the United States should assist in every way that it can. For it is clearly in our own interest that Britain become part of the Common Market.

There are, moreover, many uncertainties in the future of both the governments of West Germany and France. The peace and stability of Europe would be greatly enhanced by British entry into the European community which should create the added benefit of smoothing the way for the admission of other countries. In such an atmosphere of continually growing cooperation the standard of living of the entire Atlantic community should rise, with a resulting increase in the stability of that area.

However, there are many people in responsible positions in Washington at present who view British entry into the EEC with misgiving. They are afraid of what the increased competition from Europe will mean to American business. Once again we are taking council of our fears, rather than considering what is best for all. Those American officials who are afraid of a powerful "United States of Europe" as an economic competitor and equal political partner propose to reorganize the North Atlantic Treaty Organization so that we, hopefully, could continue to play a leading role. This has led to our trying to force on Europe such concepts as the MLF (Multi-Lateral Force), a proposal that Europe rejects.

NATO was created in Washington on April 4, 1949. The treaty provided that "an armed attack against one or more of the parties to the treaty in Europe or North

America shall be considered an armed attack against them all." The treaty has served good purpose. At the time it was signed, Europe was particularly weak and the United States had only lightly armed constabulary forces in Germany. Germany itself had nothing more than internal security forces. But again times have changed. The Common Market has brought unprecedented prosperity to Western Europe. Germany has become militarily powerful. Our own military forces remain in Europe, not so much for their actual military strength but to indicate that the United States is willing to commit major forces in Western Europe in the event of an attack.

At the beginning of NATO the United States provided of necessity the bulk of the forces, the backup of nuclear weapons and the supreme allied commander. Although in conferences and staff meetings individuals of all NATO countries spoke of cooperation and sacrifices for the common good, the fact was that the United States led and sought to influence the policies of NATO in its own interest. This attitude continues. Europeans are particularly sensitive to this because of the short period of time between the U.S. occupation of Europe and the entirely different American role as a partner in NATO. To the French in particular, the U.S. forces retained the image of an occupying power, and an unacceptable one. The French made this clear when they withdrew their own military forces from NATO.

I have had intimate and close working relationships within NATO from its beginning until I left France in 1962. I was the first Chief of Staff, Allied Forces Southern Europe, from 1951 to 1952 and also commanded the

U.S. Army Seventh Corps in Germany in 1952 and 1953. I recall that in 1952 the French sought to obtain American support for the construction of airport, highway and seaport facilities in Algeria. The French looked upon Algeria as part of metropolitan France and thus a part of the NATO area. The United States, which was providing the bulk of infrastructure funding, refused the French request on the ground that Algeria was not truly part of France and was beyond NATO's scope.

However, when the United States sought to obtain support for our own commitments in Southeast Asia, it brought the matter to the agenda of NATO. Now it was we who sought the support of our allies. It takes little imagination to understand the French resentment of this about-face of principle, particularly since Vietnam is a former French colonial area in which the United States has taken over the French role. This is but one example of the sort of irritation that disturbs the inner tranquillity of NATO. Such actions of ours cause our allies to wonder if NATO really exists to serve the best interests of all, or only of the United States.

We should have begun, in concert with our allies, to reexamine NATO in the light of today's conditions some time ago. First of all we should recognize that the Common Market is here to stay. It is already a powerful economic organization and potentially a strong political and military organization. We should encourage this community and aid the admission of such additional members as the United Kingdom. Recognizing the increasing power of the "United States of Europe," we should treat Europe as a genuinely equal partner in whatever new NATO structure may evolve. The State Department should be restrained from forcing upon Europeans U.S. views of what Europe should look like under the guise of NATO reorganization. Reestablished as a partnership among equals, NATO can deal in a cooperative way with such critical matters as the control and deployment of nuclear weapons and missiles.

THE MIDDLE EAST

In the missile age, an age we are well into now, the future security of Europe depends more upon who controls the Middle East than on whose troops are on the Danube or on the Elbe. The occupation of Morocco, Algeria and Tunisia by Soviet missile forces would spell the end of the military independence of Western Europe. The Middle East is the great land bridge that connects Europe, Asia and Africa and it is the sea bridge that connects the Atlantic and the Mediterranean with the Indian and Pacific oceans. It is the most sensitive and vital portion, geopolitically speaking, of the earth's surface.

Little wonder then that the Soviets have sought to take advantage of our preoccupation in Southeast Asia by penetrating effectively into the North African areas. This penetration began back in the mid-fifties with the Soviet-Egyptian arms deal and the cultivation of allies among other Arabic countries of the Middle East. Today the Soviets are providing substantial military assistance to Algeria, Egypt and Syria. After the Israeli-Arab six-

day war of 1967, the president of the Soviet Presidium
flew to Cairo to see President Nasser; the Russian re-
plenishment of arms, missiles and aircraft began at once.
The Soviets assigned to Cairo their top diplomat and
troubleshooter, Sergei A. Vinogradov, whose presence
makes clear their intent to not only replace the lost arms
but to build up a substantial and powerful military base
in Egypt.

It was fortunate for the United States and Western
Europe that the forces of Israel defeated the Arab forces
quickly and completely, because an Arab victory over
Israel would have meant a Soviet victory. And successful Soviet penetration of the Middle East would have
completely changed the defensive posture of Western
Europe. It is imperative, therefore, that U.S. policy
recognize the importance of the Middle East and North
Africa to the security of Europe. If we consider the
security of Europe vital to our own national security,
then a prosperous and peaceful Middle East is equally
vital.

LATIN AMERICA:
OUR NEGLECTED NEIGHBOR

The United States has never really had a positive, con-
structive policy toward Latin America. Here again we
have been reacting to daily problems rather than following a long-range plan. We are wealthier, we are more
powerful, and we have almost as large a population as all
of Latin America. Yet the so-called "realists" who con-

trol our Latin American foreign policy act most of the time as if, faced with formidable neighbors, we were under threat.

We use our military and economic strength to guard our own wealth and welfare, rather than to help provide for the well-being of the whole hemisphere. People who believe that our true national self-interest lies in the health of the entire hemisphere are considered "weak sisters" whose idealism can imperil our nation in time of crisis. To protect our own power by any means remains our paramount policy in our relations with Latin America. For short-term advantage we commit long-term errors.

For example, it is no secret that the formation of the Alliance for Progress, cited by some as second only to the Peace Corps as an idealistic intiative of President Kennedy, was to a very great extent a reaction to Castroism. Though altruism played some part it was not exactly out of the goodness of our hearts that we decided to embark upon a cooperative development effort with the Latin American sister republics. Nor was the desire to be our "brother's keeper" why we agreed to strive over a period of years to eliminate the ignorance and poverty that afflicted our neighbors to the south.

Rather than conceiving the Alliance principally as a means to prevent the spreading of Castroism, we should have sponsored it because it was the right thing to do. Castroism would have been an easy victim of a successful Alliance fully supported by our Latin partners. But we did not have wholehearted support—the Latin American nations correctly judged that we were reacting out of fear of Castroism, and not from a genuine desire to help them.

Geography has decreed that we share this hemisphere with our fellow Americans south of the Rio Grande. Political and economic relationships have developed over the years as a result of this physical proximity that necessarily binds us together. We share the "New World." It is imperative that Latin Americans and North Americans work together in a spirit of friendly, neighborly cooperation.

In spite of the visible gains which the Alliance has brought to Latin America, the area generally speaking is in a deep crisis. Military governments still control some of the more important countries; in others, quasi-military governments have been foisted on the people by questionable democratic procedures. We in the north must try to understand the critical problems that beset these neighbors, for these problems cause them to behave frequently in incomprehensible and sometimes hostile ways toward us. We must study the history of the area, the economies of the various countries, the human resources they have at their command and the political and philosophic thoughts of their intellectuals.

The intermittency of the interest we have shown in the progress of our southern neighbors and the inadequacy of some of our policies have made anti-Yankeeism a tradition in Latin America. Dislike for the United States is as much a part of the psychological makeup of a Latin American as the language he speaks; there are virtually dozens of theories as to why this is so. Therefore a first priority is research, analysis and close scrutiny of these root causes so that we know the proper actions to take. A few scholars—far too few—have undertaken this study. Unfortunately, little of their work is known or comes to the attention of the Washington policy makers.

To illustrate the extent of our ignorance, only a handful of North Americans have read *Ariel* by the Uruguayan intellectual José Enrique Rodó. Yet there is hardly a high school student, much less a college graduate, in Latin America who has not read *Ariel* several times. Seldom has articulate anti-Americanism been expressed with such force and elegance. This little book, addressed primarily to youth, has undoubtedly influenced the lives and opinions of many young Latin Americans.

The book is full of such passages as:

> The ideal of beauty does not move the United States descendant of the austere Puritans. Nor is he moved by the ideal of truth. He deprecates all exercise of thought lacking an immediate finality as being vain and unfruitful. He does not bring to science a disinterested desire for truth, nor has he ever manifested himself in any case as loving it for itself. Research is for him only the preparation for utilitarian application. . . . The religiosity of the Americans is nothing more than an auxiliary aid to criminal law. The highest point of their morals is that of Franklin: A philosophy of conduct which finds its end in what is mediocre about honesty, in the utility of prudence; from whose womb never will arise saintliness or heroism. . . .
>
> Today, they openly aspire to first rank in universal culture, to leadership in ideas, and they consider themselves the forgers of a type of civilization which will prevail. . . . They lack that superior gift of amiability,

in the highest sense, of that extraordinary power of sympathy with which the races blessed with a providential trust of education have been able to make of their culture something similar to the beauty of classic Hellene, in which everyone imagines he can recognize traces of his own. . . .

It would seem obvious that a Latin American classic like *Ariel* should be studied carefully by those who guide our Latin American policies. Yet I am told that in the library of the Department of State in Washington there is but one single volume of the book. In the fifty years since it was put on the shelves there, it has been taken out twice.

This lack of interest in how Latin Americans think and feel is reflected in the casual manner in which our country approaches the construction of its Latin American policy. Hopefully modern communications technology will make it possible for the Latin Americans to know us better and, more important still, for North Americans to know the Latin Americans better.

The attitudes and problems that emerged in the lands to the south at the end of World War II are of a piece with the political, social and economic revolution that has been sweeping the entire southern half of the world—Africa, Asia, and Latin America. In the case of Africa and Asia, the accent has been on shaking off colonialism and winning political independence. In Latin America, where twenty republics have been politically independent since the early part of the nineteenth century, the emphasis has been on industrialization and economic independence.

[86]

Latin Americans have come to realize with shocking and explosive clarity that the political sovereignty they gained one-hundred fifty years before has not brought an end to economic dependence. Cries of neocolonialism are heard in the land. Communism has not been the vital or indispensable element in the postwar crisis in Latin America. The driving force has been the burning ambition of these peoples to be citizens of politically free, economically strong (which means industrialized) and socially integrated nations.

Economically, Latin America has been principally a producer and exporter of basic primary commodities. Since the end of the Korean War, the prices of these basic commodities have suffered in the world's markets; the terms of trade have been adverse for over a decade. It is against this background that President Kennedy launched the Alliance for Progress in 1961—principally as an alternative to Castroism and violent revolution. There seems to be general agreement among Latin Americans that economic integration and a greater emphasis on manufacturing for export are necessary, but little progress has been made. At the same time our own Congress is becoming increasingly hostile to all foreign aid expenditures. We need to search out new strategies that will help the Latin Americans to achieve their own peaceful revolution.

I believe we should, over a period of time, in large measure substitute trade for aid. I propose we seriously consider giving preference to Latin American manufactures in the United States market. Lest we proceed under a misconception, let me say that neither the United

States nor Western Europe has been very liberal in its trade policies toward developing nations.

Trade liberalization has been the policy of the United States in the past decade or so; yet the establishment of lower tariffs has been limited to negotiations such as those of the Kennedy Round, which fall within GATT (General Agreement on Tariffs and Trade). The Trade Expansion Act, which authorized the Kennedy Round, did not represent a real answer to the requirements of underdeveloped countries for the elimination of barriers to their exports.

While it is true that as a result of the successful conclusion of negotiations in Geneva in 1967 there probably will be a reduction on the duties on, for example, automobiles, this reduction will benefit equally all nations who trade with the United States. An efficient manufacturer of automobiles, such as Germany, France or Britain, will be able to take greater advantage of this duty reduction than a small inefficient manufacturer, such as Brazil, Argentina or Mexico. This is why most of the underdeveloped nations of the world, and particularly the Latin American countries, are disenchanted with the notion of tariff relief via the Kennedy Round. They feel they have special problems (which they do) and that they need special help.

The United States should reconsider the position it took at Geneva during the United Nations conference on trade and development in 1964. We should study more intensely the possibility of a more liberal trade policy for Latin America, that part of the underdeveloped world toward which we have a special responsibility and to which we are tied by history and geography.

The granting of preferential tariff treatment to Latin American exports would be a far-reaching effort to close the gap between the haves and have-nots in this hemisphere. As the Latin American nations began to take advantage of the elimination of tariff barriers by exporting more manufactured goods to the United States, much unilateral economic assistance could slowly be withdrawn. This would not mean discontinuation of American participation in the financing of the multilateral financing agencies such as the World Bank, International Development Association (IDA) and the Inter-American Development Bank. Support of these agencies should be maintained at the same or higher levels so that they may continue to finance the human energy available in Latin America as it struggles to help itself.

Economic integration has been a Latin American dream of many years' standing. The most ambitious attempt at integration—the Latin American Free Trade Area (LAFTA)—has limped along for seven years without achieving mass support. The fault probably lies with the ponderous system of negotiation of commodity by commodity. Were an automatic percentage reduction of duties across the board agreed upon, full economic integration of the area could be achieved in the eighteen-year span suggested at the recent meeting of presidents at Punta del Este. The achievement of a Latin American Common Market would be of tremendous benefit to the entire hemisphere.

Turning from things we should do to things we are doing that we should not do, I am concerned that in selling sophisticated weapons to Latin America, such as the latest jet fighters, we are starting an arms race (which no one wants) in our own backyard. The arms competition among countries of the "southern cone"—Argentina, Brazil and Chile—now is extending itself to Peru and Venezuela. The acquisition of sophisticated supersonic jet fighters by one country has started a chain reaction which may siphon off hundreds of millions of dollars in arms purchases from desperately needed programs for economic development.

For reasons of prestige more than of fear, the purchase of advance armament by one country is immediately followed by still larger purchases by others. Shaky regimes fearful of antagonizing their military leaders prefer to postpone much-needed education, housing and highway programs rather than deny the military services the modern hardware they desire.

The rationale of hemisphere defense cannot be used to excuse this miscarriage of U.S. foreign policy priorities. In this age of nuclear missiles, collective hemisphere security must depend on the capabilities of the United States. Most Latin American leaders understand this, but few can resist the pressures of their military establishment and the blandishment of our Pentagon arms salesmen. And if arms are denied them in the United States, there are always other countries ready and willing to work out a deal.

Instead of fostering military acquisitions we should do what we can to prevent them. There are a number of strategies the United States could adopt to aid Latin American nations to resist the siren call of the arms salesman. It is in our long-term interest to discourage militarism in Latin America, not encourage it. A sympathetic but firm attitude on our part, plus quiet support of Latin American chief executives who work to minimize the arms race, could help put an end to this gross misuse of precious national resources.

In the past we have often been so concerned with other areas of the world that we have neglected the nations of this hemisphere, many of which have a long and vigorous democratic history. A man cannot set out to assist the world and neglect his own neighborhood. If we are one world, which I believe we are, then we are certainly one hemisphere.

SOME CONCLUDING THOUGHTS

Although the United States has long considered itself a close partner of Europe, it has also become, since World War II, a Pacific power. America has an interest in the maintenance of peace and the growth of prosperity in the Pacific area because our own security and economic growth will continue to be tied to that of the Pacific powers. Japan, particularly, has prospered with our help but still needs greater markets; we would do well to encourage the increase of her trade with Red China.

The existence of Communist China itself cannot be ignored, and her admission into the United Nations seems inevitable. We cannot continue to act as though seven hundred and fifty million people did not exist in human society. To be sure, we have a very serious problem with Taiwan, and we have a responsibility to the Taiwan government that we must respect. This will undoubtedly complicate recognition of Red China, but it should not permanently deny it.

From a military point of view the key to the security of Southeast Asia is the Philippine Islands. We have long had ties with the Philippines; these must be continued and supported and further developed. Indonesia also is an energetic and important nation with which we should maintain the closest friendship.

If we can bring about a resolution of the Vietnamese situation, it is hoped that a free, neutral, independent Vietnam can be established that will provide a buffer state between Red China and the other nations to the southeast and southwest of Vietnam. I do not believe it to be vital to our national interest to maintain a fortress area on the coast of Southeast Asia, but that we will have one there for some time as a consequence of our current Vietnam involvement seems quite clear.

Since U.S. bases on the coast of Southeast Asia are not vital, a part of any resolution of our Vietnamese involvement must envision the ultimate extrication of major U.S. forces from Vietnam. Guarantees of freedom, neutrality and independence for any new Vietnamese government should be sought through the United Nations. And problems of the independence and neutrality of Laos, Cambodia and Thailand should be handled in the same way. Any violation of these countries should be treated as a matter properly handled by the United Nations and not by the United States exclusively.

One of the most interesting innovations in foreign aid in the last few years has been the Peace Corps. The Corps has been important both for the idea itself and the people who join it. It is impossible to overestimate the impact of young, idealistic men and women, many with special skills, living in the countryside of the nations they have come to help. Particularly in the less developed countries, where there was little structure to receive more traditional forms of foreign aid, the Peace Corps has rendered exceptional service.

One of the most fascinating aspects of the Peace Corps was its creation outside the framework of civil service. A man or woman who showed ability to work with the people in the host nations could be promoted without the all-pervasive restrictions of seniority; those who were unable to master the necessary skills were fired. Many feared at the time that people would be unwilling to work without the protection of civil service. Exactly the reverse turned out to be true. Able men and women flocked to the Peace Corps, glad of the chance to serve and be promoted on their merits rather than be judged by the tedious criterion of seniority established under civil service regulations. As a pioneer in new methods of federal job employment the Peace Corps may have as much effect upon domestic America as upon any foreign government to which the Corpsmen were accredited.

After serving for two to four years, many Peace

Corps volunteers are now scattered about America, in government, universities, foundations, and private industry. They constitute a reservoir of talent and knowledge on various developing nations that the United States has never possessed before. This expertise will be invaluable in the future conduct of both our official foreign policy and the dealings of American industry abroad. For example, at a recent White House dinner for Emperor Haile Selassie of Ethiopia the only two people who could be found who spoke Amharic fluently enough to serve as interpreters were both former Peace Corps volunteers. The ability to make person-to-person contact without the language barrier has been absent too often from our foreign policy. The Peace Corps' initial sense of purpose should be regained; more, it should be encouraged and expanded.

Nations are generally touchy about receiving any form of foreign aid, even one in such good graces with some nations as the Peace Corps. One way to expand the Peace Corps' program and make it even more welcome in the host nations would be to have those nations that so wish send over their own volunteers to work in our society as part of a Peace Corps exchange. In this way the volunteers from the United States would be looked on as part of an exchange of cultural values rather than as people from a "superior" country coming to the host nation as part of an aid program. This would be psychologically helpful to Peace Corps members in their efforts to achieve a more intimate working relationship with the citizens of the countries they visit. At the same time in the United States, education in particular and society as a whole would be enriched by people from areas of the world with which we formerly had little contact.

In the nuclear age the development of the United Nations into an organization that can actively assist in keeping the peace should be a primary concern of U.S. foreign policy. For whenever the United States or the Soviet Union moves into any area of the world with unilateral aid programs or military assistance, tension is created and rivalry becomes intense. The United Nations can provide aid and a police force without the disadvantage of taking sides in the Cold War. We should encourage the U.N. to take such action for both the benefit of the world and our own self-interest.

At present the United Nations is facing something of a crisis of its own over the admission of the many small entities which have recently become nations, the so-called "micro-states." As a matter of highest priority the United States should work for a solution of this critical problem. Perhaps the answer would be some type of associate membership in which the micro-states could participate in the U.N. programs such as economic development and health without taking on the burden and responsibilities of full membership.

A particular aspect of the United Nations that has long held great interest for me is the creation of a United Nations police force. Article 43 of the United Nations Charter establishes the legal basis for such a force. Both the United States and the Soviet Union are on record as being in favor of such a police force, though they have disagreed on details of its composition and control. One of the most important strategies in keeping war limited is to keep the major powers uninvolved in any local conflicts that may occur. Here a police force operating under the United Nations could play an important role.

It seems to me that much of the debate over whether a U.N. police force would be desirable arises from a confusion as to what such a force would do. Some see such a force as large enough and powerful enough, perhaps even armed with nuclear weapons, so that it could police the major powers. Such a force is obviously impossible to create at the present time; but further, I believe it to be theoretically unwise.

Restraint in the nuclear age is a most precious virtue. On occasion both we and the Soviet Union have shown that we understand this, and we have both bowed to the demands of international justice and reality. How can we be certain that any international police force big enough to police us both would do the same? Nations that have traditionally played the role of peacemaker on the international scene have become quite belligerent once they themselves became powerful. Witness the behavior of India in Kashmir after India gained power. *Quis custodiet ipsos custodes?*—who will guard these guards? —remains a major problem.

To place the power to police the entire world in a new force created by negotiation and bureaucratic fiat, without history or tradition, would seem an unwise action. For some two hundred years of history the Roman Praetorian Guard acted as such a final arbiter of power. They had the right of arms to make or unmake the emperor. Yet this period of history, the time of Nero and Caligula, is not usually cited by proponents of an all-powerful, super-national police force in support of their argument.

However, a small, highly mobile and sophisticated police force that could step in between combatants in minor disputes would seem to everyone's advantage. In both the Middle East and the Congo such a force, had it been in existence in the past, could have acted to prevent incidents and stabilize the area. The composition, control, and scope of action of such a force would have to be determined by debate. Here is an area in which all the members of the United Nations could play a decisive part. The United States should encourage the formation of such a U.N. force.

America should also be prepared to supply any police agency created with the latest equipment in order to make the force fully effective. It is to our advantage to stop disputes before they occur; if they do explode into warfare we must do everything we can to keep them small. To enable the force to go where it wants, when it wants, and see what it wants, even at night, would have a beneficial effect on international stability. Any would-be aggressor would have to face the likely prospect that he would be discovered and beaten decisively almost before his operations had commenced.

Beating swords into plowshares or transforming nuclear explosive from weapons into electric power reactors requires time and human energy. The United Nations, torn by disputes and problems though it is, exists as a structure by which we can attempt to solve international issues. Perhaps everyone wishes that at some time over some event the United Nations had done more or acted differently. Yet, it remains the one institution that we have that can enforce some semblance of international order and before which issues can be talked out rather than shot out. We must work to strengthen the United Nations and its affiliated organizations both for our own self-interest and the interest of the world community.

V

THE HUMAN
ENVIRONMENT—
THE CITY

Domestically America has begun a new revolution. I use the word "revolution" precisely and not as a figure of speech. Unless we realize the size and nature of our problem, any answers we give will be too little and too late—and indeed quite irrelevant. Violence will increase and the overall breakdown of our national life will follow as a scientific certainty.

In the late twenties when Franklin D. Roosevelt entered the political scene the unit of explosive energy was a pound of TNT. Now the unit is the H-bomb. The speed of travel was measured by the Model T Ford; we will soon travel by supersonic jet. These two sets of relations can be written as an equation: TNT/H-bomb = Model T/Jet. We can make another ratio in which

FDR equals the social revolution started by President Franklin D. Roosevelt; and X equals where we are today. Adding this to our equation we get: $TNT/H\text{-bomb} = Model\ T/Jet = FDR/X$. Put this way it is certainly obvious that in the realm of X, our social progress, we have a long way to go to catch up to the progress in technology and the physical sciences.

The environment in which over 80 per cent of Americans live is the great city complexes sprawled across the nation. Bewildered, confused, whipsawed by the scientific revolution, we face this environment and attempt to deal with it. We have the newest tools of science in our hands. We have masses of information available on what we should or should not do. We have inventions, machines, experts, statistics, calculators. Yet the environment in which we live, instead of becoming more and more responsive to our will, swings and jumps in alarming patterns that seem quite beyond our ability to control. There is a reason for this. And that reason is basic to the understanding of our domestic crisis.

OUR ENVIRONMENT
AS A SYSTEM

Before exploring the urban crisis specifically, it is necessary to understand how the environment in which we live today differs as a whole from our past environment. For there has been a fundamental change in the way we affect our environment and how it in turns recoils on us. This change makes it vastly more difficult for us to understand and control the world around us. It forms the background of confusion, uncertainty and fear before which stands our urban crisis with its own awesome dimensions.

Before the scientific revolution, the population explosion, and the concentration of mankind in cities, the environment around us had been constant for millennia. The country was the country, and the sea the sea. Between these, man existed and made his mark. Yet beyond the small part of the planet he lived in, all was practically unchanged since the retreat of the glacial ice.

At that time our external environment was what scientists call in an equation a given or constant. The balance between animal and plant life, the weather, the energy of the sun, i.e., the ecological balance, had gone unchanged for centuries. There were chances and problems in life. In the wilderness a man might get eaten by a bear or scalped by Indians, but he knew he would not get bitten by a pine cone. When a man felled trees to build a house, or shot a deer, or laid rails across the plains, he knew the result of what he was doing because he was changing only slightly a constant, the vast pattern of nature—subtracting three from five. There were not enough of him, nor was the power of his science great enough, to upset the ecological balance in which man himself lived. He might exterminate the bison and this would affect the attitude of the Indians toward him. But these were simple relationships of the kind that had been constant for centuries. Usually they could be foreseen and understood without difficulty. Now all this has changed. The urban environment in which we live today has existed, not for centuries, but for less than half a century.

When we alter our urban environment we are not changing a system that has been stable for a great period of time. We are changing an extension of ourselves that is in the process of rapid, complex growth, and about which we have a limited understanding. We, not time and nature, have created this brief new world in which we live. And when we make changes, these changes recoil upon us in totally unforeseen ways. We spray pesticide and the birds vanish; we build a superhighway and start a riot; we extend charity and break up families; we pass a law to renew our cities and spill slums over the land.

We do not deliberately do these things because we are stupid, or evil, or enjoy riots, or hate birds, but because we do not understand the ecological balance of the vast, man-made system that is our present environment. The very studies we make of this system alter it as they are being made. This is a known fact of physical science and should not have surprised us as it has. Lacking data and understanding, we can often only make vague "guesstimates" about what may be the effect of any given action. And each action we take alters the total system in ways we do not understand and makes the next crash program more immediately necessary and more ultimately hazardous. This is the grim background against which with inadequate plans and strength we are presently trying to attack our domestic revolution.

For example, one of the solutions being advanced to

make better use of the city's scarce land is the construction of more high-rise apartments. This would increase the population density in certain areas and clear other parts of the city for parks, arts, recreation and industry. Yet in recent laboratory experiments in which rats were raised in artificially cramped quarters, the overcrowding not only broke down the rats' normal social patterns of mating, child rearing and food gathering, but also changed the rat physiologically. Their adrenal glands were enlarged and chemical differences appeared in their nervous response.

We do not know if even present levels of urban congestion are doing the same thing to ourselves. We know that enforced overcrowding of slum life creates psychological damage but what of physiological damage? And even the affluent and semi-affluent in their high-rise apartments or suburban people boxes may be more affected by population density than we realize. I don't mean to imply that this is so, but rather to cite it as an area in which we are proposing solutions without being fully aware of the consequences.

Turning from the total human environment to the cities specifically, here we find a cat's cradle of interlocking causes and effects. Among the factors contributing to the decay of our urban environment are: bad housing, discrimination, poverty, lack of jobs, poor education, complacent bureaucracy, the farm revolution. These in turn relate to such items as land values, interest rates, the tax structure, industrial policies, individual and social desires and legal precedent. To make the city's plight even more desperate, the city does not have a single, simple goal; like landing a man on the moon, or harnessing nuclear energy; but a series of goals held by different parts of its population that are often in conflict with each other.

Regulations to halt air pollution affect the locations of factories, the cost of power, law enforcement, the city's industries, job opportunities for painters, street cleaning, and the labor market generally. An improvement in urban transportation shifts populations, raises some land values and lowers others; creates opportunities to build parks, factories, slums, or schools; and by sending people to work in comfort rather than horror influences their choice of where to live. Fire regulations designed to prevent loss of life in factories of the 1920's limit the size of theaters, and set ticket prices in the 1960's. Clean water in our rivers will change the value and living patterns of vast neighborhoods, the cost of waste disposal and the tax rate. All around us actions and reactions relate to each other in ways we are just beginning to understand.

To illustrate the complex nature of the urban crisis let us look in more detail at two examples. First the relationship between rural America and the urban crisis, and second the problem of poverty. In both we see how the crisis in our cities cannot be understood or attacked except as part of the total American pattern. By examining a portion of the urban complexity we can better measure the degree of change necessary to reverse the processes of decay in our domestic environment.

THE RURAL-URBAN PATTERN

Though some would like to divide America neatly between city and farm, both are locked together. Cities cannot be considered apart from the rural life they have replaced. Between 1960 and 1970 an estimated ten million farmers will have moved to the city. The majority of these migrants, white and black, will be the poor, the underprivileged, the undereducated. Writers have described with heartbreaking eloquence the agonies of the move from Southern farm to Northern ghetto, where the streets were littered with garbage and broken promises rather than paved with gold. Bad housing, discrimination and continued poverty have been the lot of most migrants.

Statistics chronicle the extent of the move without revealing the agonies of transition. In 1910, 81 per cent of all Negroes lived in the rural areas of the former Confederate states. By 1960, 73 per cent of America's Negro population were living in cities, primarily in the North. Seventeen per cent of the population of the core cities of the North were Negroes. And two-thirds of the adult Negroes living in Northern cities had been born in the South. Such a population movement would itself have raised tremendous problems without being reinforced by discrimination and poverty.

These figures are only partly reliable. One of the grave limitations on our ability to understand and plan is the inadequacy of the census figures. The 1960 census, the most thorough in our history, now appears to have under-counted the number of people in America by some 5.7 million—an error roughly equivalent to failing to count Chicago and Los Angeles. The vast majority of those not counted were nonwhites.

Recent studies that have examined this undercount give a clearer indication of the dimensions of our urban problem. One out of every six Negro males between the ages of twenty and thirty-nine was not counted. This vast number of people had simply disappeared from the fabric of organized society, or at least from a society organized the way the census takers thought it should be. They exist in the cities, but where and how? Such a gap in our knowledge not only frustrates planning but causes injustice in the distribution of federal funds and the districting of Congress. One man–one vote requires our ability to locate the invisible man.

The driving force in this migration off the farms to the city has been the changes in agriculture brought about by science and technology. For example, between 1945 and 1955 the amount of cotton produced in Texas in-creased 13 per cent, but the farm labor decreased by 50 per cent. An estimated 60,000 Negroes are presently out of work in the Mississippi delta. Many of those in rural areas would like to stay on the farm rather than migrate but economically cannot do so. If they did move they would rather move to some nearby town where they have relatives and where customs are the same. But for the same reason there are no jobs on the farm, there are no jobs in the small town. At the same time, in ways not entirely understood, the cities exert some form of social pull: better jobs, cars, at least a change. Like entry into the hall of fame, both push and pull play a part.

There is also evidence that in some communities local politicians abuse the federal food stamp program to starve Negroes off the farms and hasten the exodus to the city. Civic groups put advertisements in local papers offering to pay the fare cityward of any Negro who wants to move. One federal government program, the Labor Mobility Demonstration Project, is actually speeding the movement of people off the farms and into the already overcrowded cities. Such bureaucratic confusion is found continually throughout the present efforts to deal with our domestic crisis.

THE UNDERCULTURE OF POVERTY

The vast majority of the migrants, both white and black, through no fault of their own, lack the education, training and job habits to fit into the complex patterns of urban life. On a farm there is so much to get done each day. The exact time each job is begun and ended does not matter. In the city you punch the clock at nine or else. This in itself is a vast difference.

The cities make few efforts to ease the entry of the new arrival into urban life. There are no special communities to receive the migrant, retrain him, place him in decent housing and find him a job. At this crucial moment of his life when a whole complex of resources should be focused to aid him, he finds himself alone.

Isolated, discriminated against, lacking the education, skills, and knowledge necessary in a highly industrialized society, bewildered by his new environment, the migrant separates from the mainstream of America and joins the undercurrent—the underculture of poverty.

The migrants join the millions already crammed into the ghettos of the central cities. They have no place else to go. In the ghetto they slowly begin to leave, if they have not already, what we like to think of as "our America." They become among those uncounted by the census. Denied participation in the American dream they become "they" and "them." So the cities—and through them the nation—tragically divide into "we" and "they." And inflaming this division to the raw edge of violence is the fact that overwhelmingly "we" are white and "they" are black.

To fully understand America's domestic crisis it is important to realize that this underculture of poverty has now gone on for so long that the Negro poor are already practically a separate society. They are not yet a separate nation with aspirations different from our own. But unless we both work together, "we" and "they," America will in fact divide more fatally than at any time in our history.

I wish there were some eloquence I could use, some fact I could cite, some verbal Pearl Harbor I could deploy, so that all Americans would rise and say, "That is true. I personally must do something about it." The riots in Watts and Detroit are there for us all to look at. A recent report to President Johnson by a White House appointed board of experts opened with the words: "You are the last President to have the option of governing one nation." I would not be that definite. But I do not believe that the report (as yet unreleased) exaggerates by much.

Inside this underculture of the poor, numbering twenty million people, white and black, the goals and aspirations of American society appear as one vast fraud. The poor know discrimination exists. They know that politically they have been denied a piece of the action. They can see the difference between their life in Harlem or Watts and the world on the TV screen. They believe, and too often experience reinforces the belief, that the police, social workers, the government, politicians and indeed anyone from the "haves" are out to keep them down or to make a buck off them. The superiority many social workers and teachers feel toward the poor is recognized immediately and hated.

Each act of discrimination, each act of violence, each magic program that remains unfunded drives the ghetto residents deeper into their world. Their belief is reinforced that they alone possess the true values in a society that they consider rotten. In the complex environment of the city we have now discovered we have been discriminating against the ghetto in ways we did not know. A new superhighway is to be built. Immediately all the neighborhoods with power in city politics begin to lobby to make certain the highway does not disrupt their lives. In the end the highway goes through the ghetto where the residents have no political punch. This recently happened in Washington, D.C., where Congressmen shifted a planned federal highway from the northwest section, where most of them live, to the northeast where the residents are mostly poor and black.

Ultimately ghetto residents come to see even genuine efforts to help them as lies and threats to their self-esteem. Those in the underculture cannot be blamed for this. Too often "improvements" have merely been words spoken by the dominant society to keep them quiet. Until the riots there was no office of the Government Employment Service in Watts. New York City has been much "improved." But there is still no shopping center or cultural center in Bedford-Stuyvesant, an area containing some 400,000 people.

All of us tend to see change as a threat. Union members often vote down company offers to study ways in which automation can be introduced to benefit both industry and labor. Some managements do not notice that a company product is growing obsolete. A man requires a sense of safety and pride to function. For the residents of the ghetto, safety is provided by the underculture. It is their pride to be poor. We have closed most other avenues of achievement to them. The goal must be to take this pride and build on it—to use the strengths and energies of the human beings in the underculture to help them gain a full life for themselves.

A particularly disturbing aspect of the underculture is the much discussed breakup of the family. It now appears that more than discrimination and poverty has contributed to this breakup; the very nature of our welfare programs has forced the poor to dissolve family ties in order to eat. (This will be discussed in more detail in considering strategies to help the family.) And when the family breaks apart, other welfare programs force the mother away from her children to earn a living.

Each time a baby cries and has no mother at home to hold him, each time a child wants food and goes hungry, each time he seeks the strength of a father and finds no father present, his attitudes toward the rewards and responsibilities of society have been shaped. If we wanted to build a system deliberately to produce nihilists, we would have a hard time devising a more efficient one than the urban ghetto we have let chance and blindness construct for us.

This is the life "we" have forced on "them." "They" have not chosen it. "They" see no way out of it and no way "they" can nourish their self-respect except by violence. This is the revolutionary situation. The gap across which we must reach to mend our severed society.

The process goes on. The gap widens. Six out of ten nonwhite children will have been supported by the Aid to Dependent Families program by the time they reach the age of eighteen. Over 600,000 people are now receiving welfare in New York City. This is roughly 200,000 more than were receiving such aid in 1941, the welfare peak of the great depression.

For the last ten years the rest of America has grown more affluent. The ghetto dwellers have become actually poorer. From 1959 to 1965 the income of a typical Negro family rose twenty-four per cent. But in Watts during that same period of time ghetto income decreased. In 1959 the median income for a Watts family had been $3,879. By 1965 it had dropped to only $3,803—and this at a time of inflation and prosperity. The same pattern is repeated in the west-central section of Cleveland. There, between 1959 and 1965 the income of an average Negro family dropped $1,758 to a low of $2,984. Imagine the quality of life these statistics of poverty and frustration reflect—a life in which three times as many Negroes as whites turn blind. "Eyeless in Gaza at the mill with slaves." Is this the Great Society?

The United States devotes a smaller percentage of its gross national product to social welfare than any other western democracy. In 1964 we devoted seven per cent of our national income to welfare; by contrast West Germany devoted seventeen per cent. We alone of the western democracies consider welfare as something to be doled out to the poor rather than as a basic right of citizenship. New civil rights legislation has been enacted, but these legal guarantees have been slow to take effect. Is this the national life we want for ourselves as a great nation?

THE WIDER CONTEXT

Though the inhabitants of the urban ghetto often find themselves outside the mainstream of American society they are not isolated from the rest of the world. Modern communications, whose importance we have already discussed, keep the ghetto residents in touch not only with members of the underculture in other cities, but also with events in the emerging nations of Africa.

Many of the nations of Africa have thrown off their old white colonial masters and now stand upright on their own black feet. The old order is changing; and as when any great structure shifts, the reverberations are felt everywhere. No longer are whites up all over the world and blacks down. Ghana, Harlem, the Congo, Algeria, Detroit are in contact by Telstar. PTA's in Watts want Swahili taught in classrooms. The Arab-Israeli war and the slaughter of Negroes by Arabs in the Sudan produce divisions on the American left.

This revolutionary change in Africa helps shape the attitude of the Negro in America. White dominance no longer exists in the world as an overriding force. Black ambassadors speak and the world listens; the President has them to lunch. Rightly, and obviously, the American Negro is not going to be content to be the last second-class citizen. Denied the usual lines of communication and power, they begin to search for ways outside the system to make themselves heard.

RIOTS

For most of us not forced to live in the ghettos, the impact of them strikes at us most directly through riots. Riots have become the most debated aspect of the discrimination-poverty-urban problem. Unfortunately the riots are often treated as if they were some isolated event and not an intimate part of the total pattern I have described.

Compressed into the ghettos of the central city, alienated from American society, lacking the cohesiveness of family, denied not merely equal opportunity but the barest stake in the future, yet offered some hope by recent civil rights advances, and strengthened by colonialism's end in Africa, a small minority of Negroes in the ghettos of America have rioted. The surprise is that most Americans were surprised. As de Tocqueville said of revolutions: "A grievance patiently endured so long as it seemed beyond redress becomes intolerable once the possibility of remedy crosses men's minds." If we doubted it before, we should realize now that there is an intolerable grievance. The question is, What are all of us, "we" and "they," to do to remove this grievance?

The reaction of the Johnson administration to the riots has been for the President to call the rioters "un-American." The President also called for respect for law and order, urged people to pray for an end to the riots, and requested Congress to increase their efforts to pass a gun-control bill. His special commission appointed to study the riots has recommended better training and integration for the National Guard. Faced with America's most total crisis since the Civil War, the administration responds with these "solutions." This could be called comedy were it not likely to lead to tragedy for all of us. Surely the administration cannot believe that prayers, name calling, billy clubs, and gun control are answers to the urban revolution.

Too often in the face of a riot, the police and the National Guard appear to have bought the dubious international doctrine of massive retaliation. Against scattered sniper fire, they put up a wall of small-arms fire that threatens or wounds the innocent, and damages the little property owned by the slum dweller. This indiscriminate response drives many ghetto dwellers into the arms of the radicals. Tanks patrol the streets, helicopters hover above, machine-gun outposts halt traffic. And the Congress shifts from passing civil rights legislation and economic opportunity programs to making moves to curb "radicals." Even a bill to deal with the serious slum problem of rats gets laughed down to defeat. This is quite literally, we must realize, a revolutionary situation.

I do not mean by this that when riots occur force should not be applied to end them. Adequate force, promptly applied with discrimination, is critical—and a test of civic leadership. I believe we should give our police more training in riot control, and certainly we should pay most of them more than we do. But these actions merely give us the opportunity to solve problems. Beyond them we must wage all-out war, not merely skirmish, with the causes of the domestic crisis.

In the past when any group rioted in America there was a time lag before others learned of the action. News of the Boston Tea Party, Shays' Rebellion and John Brown's raid spread slowly. Now electronic communications convey the news of riots across America instantly. The turf is nationwide. From Africa the Negro rioters have learned the possibility of stature; from their fellow rioters in the American ghettos they learn they are not alone.

Newspapers, television, radio and national magazines explain the techniques of successful rioting—from the preparing of Molotov cocktails to principles of guerrilla action. And sometimes, in the drive for sales, the press unfortunately plays up a riot or a riot leader beyond their importance. There is no need to look for conspiracy to explain the spread of riots. The conditions are there. And the modern communications necessary for our complex urban life spread news of a single incident of riot throughout the land, like plague spreading in a crowded city.

To me, though I know it is unpopular to say so, the similarity between the riots in our cities and the war we are fighting in Vietnam is all too obvious. In one, the guerrillas strike and disappear into the countryside that is their home; in the other, rioters strike and then disappear back into the urban ghetto, where they are nourished and protected from the police. Even those who may not sympathize with the rioters protect them out of loyalty to the ghetto and, of course, from fear. I make this analysis not to claim the rioters are Communists— that would be ridiculous—but to portray things as they are. For if we do not understand the nature of the riots and the conditions that produced them, we cannot devise plans to produce a genuine end to this threat.

I do not condone riots. I have always remembered the words of Lincoln: "There is no grievance that is a fit object of redress by mob law." Order must be maintained. Property—everybody's property—must be protected. The safety of human life is all-important. These are truisms, but no less true and important for being that.

However, I too have been an orphan, a school dropout; I have picked over mine slag heaps for coal, looked hungrily into store windows. How I wanted a bicycle! Yet my life was infinitely better than that offered by

the urban ghetto. And I was certain if I could get schooling, I could get ahead.

Riots are wrong, but I can understand what the rioters
want. And I don't mean just looted goods. They want
the opportunity to become everything they can be. So
did I. I had that chance. The ghetto dweller does not.
The Negro who finishes high school has less chance to
obtain a job than the white dropout. I could live where
I wanted. They cannot. I was judged, most of the time,
on my ability. They are not. I was paid the same as other
men for what I did and promoted as fast. They are not.
We cannot enforce order on all and deny opportunity
to some. We all require both.

People occasionally ask me why in order to attack
domestic decay it is necessary to give so much help to
the members of the underculture. Would it not be enough
to eliminate most discrimination and provide decent jobs
for all? An end to discrimination and equal opportunity
in jobs are certainly two steps long overdue. But the
analysis of poverty and its relation to urban decay has
shown that even jobs and equality by themselves are
no longer enough.

Supposing there was a foot race, and one of the two
contestants entering it had been training all his life, had
had the best of food and care, and top-flight coaching
on how to run. The other contestant was emaciated,
had never raced before, and had recently broken his leg.
An onlooker might question the fairness of the race. And
if the judges answered that the race was fair because
both men were starting from the same place when the
gun went off, the onlooker might have some further

doubts about the competence of the judges. By now, to remain one nation we have to do more than merely provide equal opportunity.

A PROCESS FOR CHANGE

I have analyzed the rural-urban environment and the riot-breeding effects of discrimination and poverty to indicate the dimensions of our domestic crisis and to demonstrate that the city's problems are not unique to the city, but extend far beyond what we traditionally think of as urban boundaries through our whole social structure. In a crisis of such size and complexity there are no simple solutions. This should go without saying, except that simple solutions keep on being advanced. But to see our domestic crisis clearly in its complexity and scope is to realize that solutions to it must also be large and multifaceted.

To attack our decaying environment we need to undertake simultaneously a series of actions, each of which is staggering in itself. We must build five million new homes. We have to end discrimination. We have to redirect our use of farm land. We have to construct a hundred thousand new schools; and provide a philosophy, atmosphere, and teachers so that all can learn. We need to provide a decent standard of living for those unable to work. We must create new social services, provide new hospitals, find more doctors, build new libraries responsive to electronic data processing, and halt the pollution of our environment.

We need to find jobs for roughly twenty million people. We must attack problems that will require vast concentrations of power to solve, without sacrificing regional difference and the uniqueness of individual people. We must create new institutions without creating new bureaucracies. Portions of the power structure of the cities, the states, and the federal government must be revitalized and reorganized. No wonder some despair while others riot. The solutions seem almost beyond human size.

I believe that never before in our history have we faced a crisis of such magnitude. The size and urgency of what must be done leads to two conclusions. First, we must make sure that the solution we are applying to this or that aspect of our domestic revolution actually will solve the problems. I don't mean that we must do everything correctly—that would be impossible. But we should understand the revolutionary situation we are in and make certain our responses fit this new situation. The crisis is too immense and time too precious for us to prescribe once again yesterday's medicines for today's ills.

Second, the response we make must be of a size appropriate to the emergency. No strategy, however correct, is going to work if applied in a small way. Challenge and response must be of the same order of magnitude, have the same scope.

If a village wishes to eradicate malaria from its midst the inhabitants must know they should kill mosquitoes and not rabbits. But they must also realize they will all have to pitch in and drain the local swamp. One boy with a fly swatter at the entrance to town will not bring the disease under control.

Having discussed the size and complexity of our domestic crisis, the next step is to examine some strategies to change it. But first let me note one basic assumption I have made. It is that we want to solve this problem, that the majority of us wish to turn this nation around. That we believe discrimination, poverty and the decay around us are unworthy of America. I have assumed that if our leaders will lead, we are not only willing to follow but that each of us will do what he can to make the task of leadership easier, that we are capable of the same sacrifices in peace to save ourselves that we have made in wars to save others. In short, we need to be led; but we are anxious to start. We do not need to be dragged.

If we wish to begin to solve our domestic crisis, how big a response is necessary? We have seen the scope of the crisis. What must be the magnitude of the process of solution? One measurement of size, not always the best one, is money. Let me use money to illustrate the amount of change I believe we need to make our environment livable for all. Later I will also measure this degree of change needed in other terms.

I propose that we take the amount of money we are now spending each year in Vietnam and add it to the amount that we now spend on ourselves. This would add to our budget for domestic improvement roughly $32 billion a year. Not all of this amount would need to be paid out each year. Some of it would take the form of tax credits, insurance guarantees, loans, and other incentives to local governments and private institutions as well as private individuals. But this addition of $32 billion indicates the approximate size of the national response I believe we must make to start the process of improvement.

At present our efforts come nowhere near this amount. For example, the federal government asked $537 million for the much-touted "Model Cities Program," and Congress appears unlikely to pass even that. Yet $537 million is a little under the amount that San Francisco alone needs to renew the substandard housing within its city limits. The programs of the Urban Renewal Agency have resulted in a net decrease in low-income housing. Such programs practice deception on the public as a whole, though the effects of the false hopes they raise fall with particular damage on those in poverty.

Economy in government is important. Having overseen economies both in government and private industry, I am well aware how attention to costs sharpens the cutting edge of endeavor. But again we must look at the present with a present eye, and not consider economy in yesterday's terms.

An unemployed member of the underculture with a family on welfare can cost the country roughly $4,000 a year. And that is only the dollar cost. The cost in human terms, a wasted natural resource, is far higher. The same human being, trained, decently housed, given opportunity for rewarding work, may in five years be earning $10,000.

Not only is the government saving $4,000; it is now collecting taxes from him. And, further, the individual contributes to society children and values that multiply his own pride and worth. People often forget this basic equation of human economics when they talk about balancing the federal budget in any given year. Private families and corporations go into debt for some time, confident of increased benefits in the future. A wise government calculates its economic policies in terms of the utilization of its human resources as well as in more classic economic terms.

We have billions of dollars invested in our cities— in buildings, communications, transportation nets and the people who live there. A private corporation which through poor policies let so much of its basic plant decay would go out of business immediately. The principle is the same here. America cannot afford to sit by and see so much of its basic plant destroyed through decay, congestion, filth, blight and riots. Bluntly, one of the reasons we need to solve our urban crisis is to protect our huge investment in the cities. The preservation of this investment must also be weighed against criticism of the expense and scope of government programs to rehabilitate our environment.

THE BASIC NEED: HUMAN ENERGY

Understanding our crisis and willing to make the response necessary, how do we begin? To improve our domestic environment the basic tool we must put to work is human energy. To link human energy to solving our crisis sounds simple, but few understand how to use the tool. To devise means to liberate human energy and link it to the process of providing solutions for our domestic crisis requires invention, intelligence and flexibility—and that not-always-present willingness to accept rather than reject new ideas. To liberate and harness our domestic energy and use it to end our urban crisis is a more gigantic task than harnessing nuclear energy in World War II.

A great deal of human energy is now being expended on the Vietnamese war, but beyond that, we waste this vital national resource in a number of other major ways. Much human energy is locked into the ghettos of the central city or exists in patches of rural poverty, virtually unable to make its presence felt except by riot. Other energy reservoirs are trapped without outlet in the bureaucracy, administering obsolescent programs that often damage the society they are meant to benefit. Even where able officials try to start change, tradition and legal and institutional barriers often prevent action.

Though some sections of private enterprise have responded energetically to the challenge of improving America, others still regard domestic decay as someone else's problem. Everywhere in our society we need strategies and inventions to free human energy and direct it in the attack against our blighted environment.

I cannot overemphasize the importance of our need for strategies, inventions and new processes to create change. One thing we do not need is more programs. We have plenty of programs. To mention just a few: Vista, the Teacher Corps, Model Cities, Rural Relocation, Vocational Education, Elementary and Secondary Education, Headstart, Follow Through, Compensatory Education, busing, MDTA, OEO, Job Corps, Youth Corps, Concentrated Employment Program, Hospital Building, Medicaid, a bewildering variety of housing programs, Urban Renewal, Public Housing, Moderate-Income Housing, Rent Supplements, Antipoverty, Community Action, Aid to Dependent Children, Welfare, Food Stamps, and many others. The very number of programs, plus the severe financial restraints under which they labor, prevents them all from reaching full effectiveness.

We need to start change now, and then provide ways for that change to snowball. One aspect of problem-solving we learn from science is that the first steps generate both fresh problems and fresh ideas and possibilities for new solutions. We cannot begin to see what these are until we start to attack a problem. In outlining several strategies to link human energy with solutions for our domestic crisis, I am not proposing new programs. I am indicating ways in which the process of change may be started. Any invention we construct today to put human energy to work will hopefully be obsolescent in two or three years as we begin to make progress. New bureaucracies and programs are what we do not want. They will merely place more barriers between human energy and the attack on our crisis.

I have no complete solutions to the decay of our environment. I would be foolish to claim to. Details will evolve and inventions take shape as we move to meet the problem. Further, as will be discussed later, it is essential that those involved in the process of change take part in the creation of the solutions that will affect their lives. To hand out solutions to those in the ghetto is as degrading as handing out charity. Their energy is a vital part of the process of change. What I wish to do is indicate a few strategies that will nourish new ideas and free energies that can start the process of change. We must beware of our American love for large organizational solutions in domestic as well as foreign affairs.

It may be of interest to consider a typical "organizational" solution. In an effort to prevent more riots we can take the structure and functions performed by an average city and break them down. Police, sanitation, education, fire control, ports, construction, welfare, courts, jobs, road building, etc. We can then devise new programs for each department involved to help prevent riots. Perhaps we can even devise a new department to coordinate all the other departments in the matter of riot control. This would take quite a lot of time, energy and skill. In the Watts riot, for example, the California highway department would be found to be a key factor. A program would have to be designed for it so that highways would not be bulldozed through places that would cause riots.

All this would be the wrong approach. What is needed is a strategy to break down the divisions between the various departments, to liberate the energies inside them, and make them all more responsive to the needs of all the people in the city.

THE NEIGHBORHOOD
DEVELOPMENT CORPORATION

To solve the problem of urban decay all the people and institutions of the city government and private industry must be involved. The task cannot be left to the schools, or the welfare department, or the housing department, or private charity, or government or private capital. The key group whose energies must be involved in the solutions of their own problems is the ghetto dwellers themselves. They do not want to be handed solutions to their problems without any say, any more than anybody else. One of the major causes of the Newark riots was a plan to locate the new campus of the New Jersey College of Medicine and Dentistry in the slum area. This campus would have been beneficial to the ghetto, upgrading the area around it and providing desperately needed medical services to the community. But the ghetto residents had not been consulted. They merely saw their homes and businesses being demolished. No one had taken the time to explain to them the future benefits, much less consult them about where it would be best to put the campus or what it should look like.

Recently in Roxbury, a suburb of Boston that was the scene of riots in 1967, the state and local governments persuaded a major firm to locate a new light-industry plant in the ghetto area to provided desperately needed jobs. When the residents learned the plant was coming, government officials expected cheers. Instead, the neighborhood organized to block the plant's arrival. Again no one had asked the residents whether they wanted the plant, where it should go, what its hiring policies should be; nor had any of its construction contracts gone to local firms. Had the company been moving to a wealthy Boston suburb it would have spent a great deal of time meeting with local community leaders, submitting plans to neighborhood groups and generally treating the residents as people of power. The ghetto residents want the same kind of power; they wish to be listened to without having to resort to riots.

The Neighborhood Development Corporation is one new agency that has shown strength in liberating and mobilizing the energies of the ghetto to solve urban problems. Though containing many unique concepts and modern features, the corporation can also be viewed as the inheritor of the old political power of the ward and the ward boss and as following the traditional path by which group after group has been assimilated into American society.

Basically the Neighborhood Development Corporation is a new political force within the city. It draws on the energies and abilities of the local people for its strength and provides a structure for the social, economic and political organization of small units within the city. In new form it deals with the old problem of the democratic control of power. The design of the corporation should permit it to receive funds from the federal and local governments as well as from private sources, make basic decisions about what happens within its political boundaries and, to put it bluntly, enable those in the ghetto to get a piece of the economic and political action.

Though designed primarily to liberate energies in the ghetto, the Neighborhood Development Corporation indicates a process that could be of benefit to all of us. From the city proper to the affluent suburbs all of America suffers from uniformity and lack of local political choice. Few of us have the say we would like in the design of our homes, the power of the local police, the education of our children, or even such a simple matter as the location of street lights.

We are all aware that we have lost a large measure of control over the environment immediately around us. Government more and more gives us things, while we influence less and less what we get. We "take" rather than "participate." Urban sprawl, pollution and uniformity blight the landscape. We have created a landscape where, as Gertrude Stein described it, "There is no there, there." Local control, for all but a few, is a shibboleth rather than a reality. The citizens of Chilmark, Massachusetts, some 180 of them, vote on how much the police chief will be paid, when the roads will be repaved, and the tax rate per acre. The citizens of Chicago, Los Angeles, Boston and New York do not. Not just in the ghetto, but throughout America, we are all becoming in certain ways politically impoverished.

In the nation's early years, the farm economy days, politics and local discussion filled a large portion of a man's time. The Lincoln-Douglas debates are rightly legendary. By foot, horse and wagon, people poured into the towns where the debates were taking place—to hear, judge, question and decide, taking an intimate part in the process of government. When a new town hall was to be built, or the streets widened, or a school teacher advertised for, the matter was discussed and voted on. If in our attack against our domestic crisis we can bring about a revival of local democracy, this will be one of the most exciting products of environmental change.

With the Neighborhood Development Corporation providing the means, local residents can now take part in the process of changing their environment. If a business wants to construct a plant in the neighborhood, its officers would deal with members of the corporation. The corporation would make certain that local officials had some say in the plant's policies, that local contractors got used in the construction, that local businessmen supplied the plant with goods and services, that local banks handled the plant's business—in short, it ensures the plant's conformity to neighborhood standards. The corporation would see to it that the ghetto in Harlem and Greenwich in Connecticut would get the same political and economic treatment.

Ethnically based businesses and ethnic political power have been the traditional American way out of the ghetto. Here Black Power is already taking a leadership role. In many areas Black Power and Black Capital have begun the process of liberating the ghetto from a handout economy. Black Power is human energy. The Neighborhood Development Corporation provides a structure to assist this energy as it produces changes within the ghetto; it not only opens up a future but gives those in the neighborhood control over that future. In this way the former members of the underculture become contributors to the nation. "We" and "they" have a joint stake in "our" future. The energies, ideas—and the tax money—from the ghetto contribute to the mainstream of American life.

One of the most successful of the pioneer Neighborhood Development Corporations is ECCO (the East Central Citizens Organization) in Columbus, Ohio. First organized as a neighborhood foundation to receive funds and run its own community center, ECCO has become an economic and political force in Columbus. With ECCO, residents of a blighted area have demonstrated their ability to control and manage their neighborhood and lives with great success.

One of ECCO's first programs illustrates how impossible it is for distant bureaucracies to even be in the same ball park as neighborhood needs. In discussing what local projects needed to be done immediately, the ECCO community decided a highest priority should go to free rabies shots for all neighborhood dogs and cats. This priority—the focus of human energy in this specific direction—made perfect local sense. The area was rat-infested and almost all the local residents had large dogs or cats. The area also had a great number of children. There had been several cases of rabies and the residents were concerned. No bureaucrat located in City Hall, and certainly none as far away as Washington could possibly have identified rabies shots as a number-one local need. Nor would another neighborhod want to put its energies into such a program.

Later the ECCO community refused the gift of a government-financed health center. The residents liked neither the design nor the proposed location of the proffered gift. Instead, with their own funds they bought title to an old house in the community that had belonged to a doctor who during his life had treated many of them decently. They turned this building into a health center as a memorial to him, finding and hiring the necessary medical equipment and staff themselves.

Neighborhood Corporations such as ECCO are themselves in the process of change and development. This is precisely what the forecast of a successful attack on our domestic crisis called for: initiative that snowballs. Among future strategies that look promising is a proposal that the Neighborhood Corporations be given the authority to issue tax-exempt bonds guaranteed by the federal government. The Neighborhood Corporation could then finance its own local improvements.

Here the strategy is to move private capital and federal funds into the ghetto area to supplement the human energy at work there. The Neighborhood Corporations could then buy local buildings for rehabilitation, and after improving them, either run them themselves as low-income housing or sell them to local private individuals. The money thus generated would pay off the interest on the bonds and provide the corporation with further working capital.

Several other areas of present controversy between neighborhoods and the central government are control over police and education. Here again are problems to which the energies of the Neighborhood Corporation could make a powerful contribution. The leaders of the corporation can negotiate for the neighborhood with the wider community. They can participate in devising standards for the whole urban environment. For it is important to have some uniform city-wide and nation-wide standards. We do not want to perpetuate the ghetto under the guise of increased neighborhood control.

All of us want our community to run the way we wish. Starting with the interior of our house and radiating outward into the neighborhood, the city, the state and the nation, we like to see our personal ideas and ideals incorporated into our environment. We all want a place somehow different, somehow ours. The free interplay between our various wants creates the excitement and life of democratic politics. The Neighborhood Development Corporation gives local citizens a chance to make their needs and wants felt inside the structure of national politics. It provides a process whereby local initiative can be used to check and direct the pervading sprawl of centralized bureaucratic power.

I see the relationship between the Neighborhood Development Corporation on one hand and the wider centers of power such as the city, private industry, labor unions and the federal government on the other as that between a shopper and a supermarket, the Neighborhood Corporation being the shopper, and the city, federal government, or an organization being the supermarket. Inside the supermarket are displayed a vast variety of brands and wares; many of them are nationally advertised; others the shopper has heard about from friends, or gained knowledge of them through trial and error. The goods on the shelf have had all the benefits of systems analysis, modern production methods and scientific research. The buyer has been placed under some pressure to buy this or that brand, but the ultimate choice is up to the shopper.

In the supermarket the shopper enjoys some protection. Pure food and drug laws and truth in packaging regulations prohibit gross forms of adulteration and mislabeling. The meat has been inspected, and the canned goods must satisfy certain standards. Should slipshod production make the goods harmful, the consumer has further legal recourse. Local laws protect him from overcharging. But these are protections rather than restrictions; and the choice remains the shopper's. His or her energies and insights are going to select the goods that get off the shelves and are used in the home. In such a way the Neighborhood Development Corporation gives neighborhoods a choice of programs. It also gives them more: the economic and political power to demand that the market stock new types of goods.

A STRATEGY FOR BUILDING

Now we turn from the process of focusing human energy in the local area to finding a strategy to attack a problem that is nation-wide. To revitalize the urban environment we must build five million new homes, a hundred thousand new schools, new community centers, industrial parks, theaters, museums, stores. But the paramount need is for homes and schools, designed attractively and located in the necessary place. How are we going to provide the national energy to accomplish this miracle of construction?

No single private or political unit, federal, state or city, has the power or scope to meet this aspect of the domestic challenge. Many of them have tried with the best will in the world, but they have not succeeded. The city cannot do it; it lacks the legal power to acquire land outside its own boundaries, the tax base to raise the necessary funds, the glamour to attract the necessary talent, the power to force the construction industry and the building-trades unions to mend obsolescent practices for the public good. Similarly no existing private corporation can command the power or the capital necessary to accomplish such a vast project.

The federal government is one of the causes rather than a possible help in the present crisis. For a series of complex sociological reasons the energies of the federal bureaucracy are directed toward increasing the power of bureaucrats rather than improving the American environment. Overly copious federal regulations make it extremely difficult, if not impossible, to apply the benefits of modern technology to construction. Seeing the failure of centralized federal power to significantly better the present environment, the country as a whole is turning away from federal intervention as the customary "best" solution.

The housing situation is one of our most desperate problems. The continued shortage of housing creates slums and fosters discrimination. To act with sufficient energy to solve the housing problem we need to end the tired debate about the public versus the private sector, or liberal versus conservative methods. The sixties are not the twenties; we now live in a mixed economy. The debate between those who believe that private industry is always bad and federal intervention always good or that the federal government is always wrong and private industry is always right has ceased to have meaning. What we need are new inventions. New ways to attack our urgent problems. To solve the housing crisis we need to join skills and energy from both the public and private sectors.

The Post Office is a government department; the telephone company a private corporation (something unthinkable to a European). The telephone company functions with an efficiency that makes other nations envious, while the postal service of many European countries is superior to our own. This suggests that neither type of ownership or supervision is necessarily superior to the other. Therefore one strategy of attack against the housing shortage could be a combined effort of government and industry to create a Special Purpose Corporation. Such a corporation would be a mixed public and private company formed for social purposes. In structure the Special Purpose Corporation would be somewhat similar to the Communication Satellite Corporation (COMSAT), for example. It would exist not merely to maximize profits but to rehabilitate the environment. It is the outgrowth of recent trends in this country. For there has been an increased tendency in the government to bypass entrenched bureaucracy and look to the corporation as a source of highly sophisticated technoplanning and managerial skills to accomplish such diverse ends as building missile systems or retraining the hard-core poor. At the same time corporations have come more and more to realize that mere profit is an inadequate measure of a human organization.

Created with the help of the federal government, but independent from it, this particular Special Purpose Corporation for housing would combine the management skills and flexibility of private industry with the scope, and in part the funds, of the federal government. I would name such a corporation URBX, or Urban Experimental Corporation. The word "experimental" is used to stress that URBX is primarily a strategy to attack the urban construction problem and not a new entity that is to live forever. In addition to attacking the problem of housing, URBX would serve as a model for other special purpose corporations that might be created to bring about change in other areas of national life.

The size and scope of URBX would permit it to shatter many of the barriers now blocking progress in the construction of housing. Energy now frustrated by these restrictions would be released. The on again–off again job situation in the construction industry would be stabilized by building a guaranteed number of housing units each year. The number of these guaranteed units would provide both industry and unions with incentives to modify present restrictive practices. URBX could buy land outside the city for new towns, create performance criteria so that new technological approaches could be used in building; and provide the cities with such an incentive to participate in the building program that they would be willing to modify obsolete local statutes. At the same time, through guaranteed loans and insurance programs, URBX could draw on the energies of private capital across the nation.

Cost analysis indicates that, permitted to benefit from

new technology, URBX could in five years reduce the cost of a $16,000 home to $8,000. In the same period of time housing units that now must economically rent for $134 a month could be rented for $67 a month.

Recently in California a systems approach to school construction agreed to by business and labor reduced in six months the cost of school ceilings from $3.24 per square foot to $1.81 per square foot. Costs for other units on which agreement could be reached were also reduced substantially. The new schools were more beautiful and flexible than previous models, and the overall cost was reduced by $1.50 a square foot. Here the link-up of human energy and school construction not only solved the construction problem; it produced savings to buy improved education for everyone.

When we create a nation-wide process to begin to solve a problem as large as the construction of housing and schools, we encounter a basic problem—one that is currently the subject of much study. The problem is: How do we keep any necessary new organizations flexible and responsive to fresh change? Good intentions are an inadequate guard against the hardening of bureaucracies and the corruptions of power. Any attack on our domestic environment must have built into it a system of checks and balances so that strategies can change as need changes. This is an old concept, as old as our Constitution, but one recently often neglected.

Both local political units, cities and states, as well as the Neighborhood Development Corporations, have important roles to play in keeping power decentralized in whatever construction system we adopt. As our environment improves, the bulldozer blade of progress will bite into the lives of many of us. The more say we all have about when and how, the more our national energy will be devoted to assisting rather than thwarting the new construction we all need.

MANHATTAN PROJECT II

This chapter began by pointing out that the world around us, the urban environment we ourselves have created, contains many unknowns. Things happen and we are not quite certain why. The Urban Renewal Act to improve cities instead spilled slums across the land. We are unsure of such diverse elements of modern life as the physiological effects of varying population densities, the best education for young children, the most economical methods of waste disposal. As we begin to construct processes to make change possible, we will find out we need to know a great deal more about factors that today seem self-evident. We need to have a pool of talent and energy upon which those in the process of change can draw for help.

Many Americans have a great deal of wisdom about our domestic environment but they are dispersed—in government, industry, the foundations and universities. Many able people drift off to work on other problems for lack of money or career incentives. Others duplicate one another's work, or spend frustrating hours on problems recently discovered data could simplify. We need to marshal a portion of this talent and energy in one place and provide the time and the physical equipment for scientists from various disciplines to help contribute to the process of urban change.

This pooling of scientists to help link human energy to social change would be similar to the mobilization of scientists in World War II to apply nuclear energy to warfare. That organization was known as the the Manhattan Project; and I believe we should call the marshaling of scientific effort to help solve our domestic crisis Manhattan Project II. This will show that we are as serious about improving our domestic environment as we were about creating nuclear weapons. And also that we realize halfway measures inside existing organizations will not be enough.

Again I am proposing a strategy of attacking our urban problem and not advocating the creation of an organization that will duplicate the first Manhattan Project in every particular. We need to provide a means to link scientific effort as efficiently as possible to the attack against the decay of our domestic environment. The exact number of scientists necessary, their location and method of organization will be determined as the process of change begins to operate.

There is a need to formulate goals and timetables; to gather data and establish controls so that the effectiveness of various programs can be measured against each other. Those involved in the process of change—the federal government, cities, states, special corporations, private corporations, and foundations—need a pool from which they can draw individuals with special knowledge and skills to help them. The rest of us will benefit from an outside evaluation of their claims of how they are doing.

Already small groups of scientists have begun to work together on their own to help social change. MARC (Metropolitan Area Research Council) in New York and OSTI (Organization for Social and Technical Innovation) in Cambridge are examples. Manhattan Project II would provide the means for a wider grouping of such talents. Architects, sociologists, anthropologists, case-workers, systems experts, economists, physicians, chemists, structural engineers, urban planners, traffic experts, economists, historians, psychologists, internists, computer programmers and others would all be brought together to give the full benefit of their combined energies and skills. We marshal the scientists necessary to land a man on the moon; we should do the same with those able to help the process of environmental improvement.

These scientists must be free to describe a whole series of alternative solutions that different cities or neighborhoods may wish to apply. We cannot be sure what will work best, but this should not surprise us, for it is part of the method of scientific discovery. Manhattan Project I built two completely different varieties of nuclear weapons before deciding on which to concentrate production. Manhattan Project II may offer five or six different approaches to the urban crisis. Such variety and competition will be another action that will stimulate improvement and change.

Perhaps some of those in Manhattan Project II will produce charts of what we wish our cities and therefore ourselves to be like in the future. Not detailed blueprints for action (the process of change will generate those of itself) but dreams of what we might like to become. New Jerusalems among which we could choose. "A great city," said Walt Whitman, "is that which has the greatest men and women." One measure of men and women is the size of their dreams.

The beauty of many ancient European towns is legendary. Their style and proportion come in large part from the central role of a church from Zeus through Roman Catholic during the time of their creation. We too need a dream, a concept of what we are, at the heart of plans for our environment. Or for all our efforts, we may wind up creating new ugliness, new slums and new uniformity, to replace the old.

A PERSONAL BELIEF

To transform our decaying American environment will be long and difficult. In comparison with our domestic crisis, Vietnam is simple. I hope I have been able to show the size of our environmental problem and the need for a revolution in thought and processes if we are to attack the problem successfully. Since I am urging that we as a nation take far-reaching action to solve this crisis, I think it important to say what I believe.

I believe in excellence for all. I believe the full life belongs to every citizen as a birthright. I believe we should abolish poverty not out of charity but because poverty shames us as a nation. I believe we should totally end discrimination not to "be nice to Negroes" but because prejudice kills the dream we could all become. I believe we should house everyone decently because in a great nation all men live well. While in a nation where some fatten while others starve, none sleep sound.

I want to abolish "we" and "they." To have both white and black become "we." The "we" of *e pluribus unum* (from the many, one). I wish to establish that unity we dreamed of when we wrote: "We hold these truths to be self-evident: that all men are created equal. . . ." We can dismiss these fourteen words as merely words. If so, we should stop harking back to them and admit our truths are bigger cars and flakier apple pies —for some. Or we can make those words the goal and purpose of our national life. We do not need new political catch phrases, or new definitions of what America is or Americans are. The dream was clearly stated in our beginning. To live the dream remains our challenge. All we need do—but all is terrifyingly large—is make those fourteen words this nation's purpose—the truth we live.

Our critics charge that we have grown too soft, too affluent, too selfish and self-centered to find our purpose again. I do not believe this. Historically we have been at our best on the frontier or in time of peril. The hydra-headed problems of poverty, discrimination and urban decay are certainly the greatest challenge we have yet faced. But let those who, appalled by the size of our present crisis, count us out remember our moments of defiance and triumph in the past. For we too have not yet begun to fight.

VI

THE HUMAN
ENVIRONMENT—
THE PEOPLE

W e have been discussing strategies that affect the
environment of people in large units, from the
neighborhood to the nation. We also need to
examine processes that benefit both the individual himself and the family life immediately about him. Again
I am not proposing detailed, specific programs but providing examples of methods and strategies by which we
can begin to change and improve the lives, not just of
those in poverty, but of all of us. Once again the key is
to release human energy to produce change. Again it
should be stressed that all those affected by any change
should have a say in how the changes occur.

Programs to improve the immediate, personal life of
people and families cannot wait. Our domestic crisis has

us on the defensive. We face the same problem as in any battle that has started badly. First we must stop things from getting worse, then take the offensive in certain vital areas, while we set in motion strategies and inventions for broad victory. But we need some immediate, visible gains in our domestic crisis, not alone for the tangible benefits they will produce but also because such victories will demonstrate that further change will come and that we are in the battle to stay.

The strategies we adopt to benefit individual people and the first victories we achieve also have importance because in the complex system of the cities initial changes can make later action much harder or much easier. As has been stressed, our present environment is so complex we cannot foresee all the results of any single action. (Those that started the Aid for Dependent Children program in the 1940's did not foresee that it would become an instrument to break up families in the 1960's.) Any new strategies must be well planned to begin with, far better planned than most existing programs. But they must also be responsive to change so that they themselves can shift as our society changes.

I again stress the need for responsiveness to change and for feedback into the system because frankly we face here a side of the American character that bothers me. There is a great deal of evidence (Vietnam is a case in point) that while we Americans do many things well, we do not admit our mistakes well. Politicians strive to clean up the record to prove consistency; bureaucrats once committed to a program will follow it to hell's end —in some of the present welfare programs operating in the ghettos they have been doing precisely this. In some sections of the building-trades industry obsolete programs and practices are maintained that damage both themselves and the economy.

We cannot afford the luxury of continuing in this way. We live in the age of the scientific revolution. Progress in science is made by experiment, through testing theory, by trial and error. In this age of rapid change forced on us by science, either we adopt an experimental posture, admit errors when we make them and adapt, or the environment around us will continue to decay. And the fierce horror of our uncontrolled cities will multiply.

As we battle to master our domestic crisis there will be disappointments, temporary defeats, struggles and even more violence. In this revolutionary situation, making changes with the speed required, we are not going to win them all. We must not let this deter us from our commitment to change. I can be no more eloquent here than the late President Kennedy:

> For only with complete dedication by us all to the national interest can we bring our country through the troubled years that lie ahead. Our problems are critical. The tide is unfavorable. The news will be worse before it gets better. And while hoping and working for the best, we should prepare ourselves now for the worst.

These words were spoken while the country was moving forward. Now, after the years of neglect, the outlook is darker and deadlier. This is a harsh thought, but we must speak truth to ourselves. When we bury our problems beneath slogans and campaign oratory they explode in violence. We must admit our mistakes and problems and take pride that we can recognize and attack events of such magnitude. Then "the troubled years that lie ahead" will find us not frightened but resolute.

My [thoughts] were of trouble
And mine were steady
So I was ready
When trouble came.

TAX STRUCTURE CHANGE

One of the most vital strategies to follow in halting the deterioration of our cities is to take an existing governmental process that is working against us and make it work for us. The federal, state and local tax structures, as they presently operate, instead of improving our environment work to build the urban ghetto. For a good home in the suburbs in a "safe" neighborhood the affluent and even the semi-affluent can obtain mortgages. Another arm of the government, the Federal Housing Administration, will reach out and insure these mortgages, as long as the building is not a slum dwelling. The interest on the mortage, the rent the affluent pay, is tax-deductible; the rent the poor pay in the slum is not.

Home ownership is something society quite rightly should encourage. A home of one's own is an important part of family life. But there should be special mortgages available, backed by government funds, that would encourage home ownership and development in and at the edges of the ghetto, and tax bonuses could well be awarded for owning in such areas.

At present, cities levy property taxes on the house rather than on the land. The immediate reward for any slum-property owner who acts to improve his property is higher taxes. After this penalty, which is as certain as taxes, his other financial rewards are far less sure. Building improvements in ghetto areas must be encouraged by special tax abatements for those willing to undertake the job. A tax program that would encourage rather than paralyze needed buildings should be developed. Changes that make life better for all city dwellers should be rewarded, not penalized.

The tax structure works the same way for industry. Federal programs encourage, often with federal funds, urban communities to zone themselves to attract desirable light industry. Local suburban communities can offer the proper desirable industry highways to its door, an industrial park and, above all, special tax rates and bonuses that make the pasturage for industry much greener— tax-dollar greener—in suburbia. This moves jobs, good white-collar jobs, out of the city and into the suburbs.

We may be in a "war on poverty" as we announce, but some of the soldiers are being given bonuses for shooting the wrong way. The federal tax program should be structured in such a way that industries that locate in depressed or near-depressed areas receive significant tax reductions for doing so. In this way companies looking for a tax break will actively seek locations in the urban depressed area rather than actively look to avoid them.

A strategy of tax change could act immediately and efficiently to provide better homes and jobs. It would avoid the creation of a new federal program with the resulting bureaucracy. Basically it provides an incentive for private capital and energy to start immediately to improve the environment and climate in the ghetto. Changes in the tax structure can be made without any increase in federal expenditures. (While this is not the yardstick of a successful program, it is a fact occasionally of interest to Congress.) It should be stressed that while strategies such as these will have immediate success, they in themselves do not come close to being the whole answer.

AN INCENTIVE FOR PEOPLE

Groups with special needs and political power have long been able to write special benefits for themselves into the tax program. Sometimes these tax bonuses have stimulated industrialization, research and the cultivation of new skills to greatly benefit the whole economy. Others have been of more dubious value. The poor, who have needs but lack political power, have been unable to gain any benefits from the federal tax program. Indeed, the poor carry a large portion of the antipoverty tax burden themselves. So the group gaining least from the tax program is the very group most in need of benefits.

Another tax strategy to solve the decay of people in our cities would be a variety of inducements to private industry to employ, not merely provide jobs, but employ, the chronic unemployed and underemployed. We have tax concessions designed to stimulate development of such vital physical resources as oil and uranium. We need an incentive to encourage development of our greatest national resource—people.

Corporations should receive substantial tax benefits for every member of the hard-core poor that they employ. Such benefits might well take the form of a double deduction for all wages, training programs and fringe benefits provided for the former unemployed man or woman. Not only does such a strategy make it advantageous for the corporation to recruit among the chronic unemployed, it would also be a great incentive for the corporation to train these individuals for progressively more important jobs. A broom-pushing job at $70 a week would merely give the corporation a deduction of $140 a week. But that same individual trained to be a $8,000-a-year junior executive or data-process technician would bring the corporation a deduction of $16,000 a year. And the cost of his training has also been subject to the same liberal tax write-offs.

Once again the purpose of such a strategy is to avoid the direct entry of the government into the lives of people. The poor do not want this any more than the rest of us. Indeed they probably want it less, for they have fewer defenses to marshal against abuses of power by the government. The private sector of the economy is encouraged to move into the poverty area and act. The result would benefit all of us.

THE ALL-IMPORTANT JOB

America cannot become great until everybody has an opportunity to support himself. We need job opportunity for all now. The shifts in the tax structure will provide some jobs. As URBX and other strategies, inside the government and without, begin to shift dirt and raise buildings improving the environment, other new jobs will be created. But in the meantime there must be jobs now.

At present we offer the urban and rural poor many promises, some money and much advice; but the all-important jobs are not forthcoming. Vast numbers of the poor desperately want an adequate job, but we have no strategy to link the individual who wants to work with work. And this does not mean a job offered as charity, but a job extended as a right.

It is not enough to have the jobs just vaguely there. To break the underculture of poverty requires effort to bring people and jobs together. Many of the people who want jobs lack the skills, education and work habits necessary in our complex urban society. They must be motivated and trained. The bulldozer mechanic and the section chief both require special training and skills. And they work under different constraints and pressures than they did back on the farm.

Both industry and government must have well-staffed recruiting and training programs. The importance of schooling in special skills is so great it will be dealt with separately in discussing education. What is important to stress now is that training should have two goals. It should prepare people for the jobs available and for jobs they want. The strategy of neighborhood participation is again critical. The poor deserve freedom of choice, subject to the same limitations as everyone else. Far too often job-training programs have been dictated by what a middle-class, slightly inefficient bureaucracy believes would be "good" for the poor—without consideration of the labor market or the future employee's desires.

As a last resort, it is necessary that the federal government stand ready to supply the necessary jobs, perhaps for a brief time as many as four million, depending on how fast other strategies come into action. At first glance this may seem to be that favorite bogyman of some, "the gigantic give-away program." But look around us at the unfinished business of our society—the schools unbuilt, the slums uncleared, the children unfed, the hospitals unstaffed, the countryside unclean, the streets unsafe. This nation does not have to endure such mountains of unfinished work.

At the same time when we have so much that should be done we also have unemployed who want jobs. To join the two to enlist in the attack on the desolation of our urban land is no give-away program. It is a do-away strategy. And it does away not only with much of poverty but with the "we" and the "they."

Here fortunately the systems nature of society works for us. Economists worry that under conditions of full employment America's productive capacity to produce may outstrip the ability of people to buy and consume. The result of this would be overproduction and quite possibly depression. But there are roughly forty million people in the United States living in or close to poverty. They are a great untapped market. To increase the buying power of these individuals is to stimulate the whole economy. We are one nation. Economically we are all in the same boat.

MONEY

Even with a strategy of full employment, we must recognize that there are some who cannot work. This is frankly a difficult and controversial problem. Those unable to work will include the blind, the aged, the psychologically unfit and the ill; also those female heads of impoverished households whose childen are too small to be left alone. At present, both on the farm and in the city, these people lead blighted lives. What payments they receive are inadequate. Much of the time a host of social workers pry into their lives to see if they are spending wisely what they receive, if they need it as they claim, and if they are living at their given address in company with those they have named. The average American would not tolerate such snooping into his personal life. Why should one particular group of society?

Previously we have looked at both the rural-urban system and the problem of poverty in some detail to illustrate the dimensions and complexity of our urban crisis. In the same way it is necessary to look at aspects of our welfare program to discover how federal and local civil service bureaucracies have failed. To begin with, there is a confusion as to purposes, programs, organization and goals, arising from confusion over what cures poverty. Do those in poverty need more counseling, more psychological help, more guidance or other such service programs? Or do those in poverty need a job? Or is the major need money? And if so, how do those in poverty get money and under what conditions? These three, money, jobs and services, jumble together in thought, articles and programs, with supporters of particular programs defending this or that as most important. Now one program, now another, is thrust on the ghetto without consulting the "beneficiaries" as to what they want. The controversy becomes most violent when it comes to giving those in poverty money.

It seems to me the confusion over giving money to cure poverty arises basically from a view held by many people that being poor is immoral; that the poor are shiftless people who just won't help themselves. If a bureaucrat dealing with the poor holds this view, it is next to impossible for him to administer a program effectively, however much he may try to hide his basic belief from himself and others.

We all of us to some extent tend to see the poor as the dark side of ourselves—as people who deliberately spend all their time drinking, wenching, and raising Cain instead of working. We see them not as victims of society but as people who choose poverty to spite the rest of us. Far too many bits and pieces of this attitude are found among those civil servants whose job it is to aid those in the ghetto and others in poverty.

Admittedly a few of the poor are no-good bums.

There are no-good bums among the rich. Even the Congress of the United States and the United States Army, two groups with which I have had long, intimate association, are not exclusively composed of saints. But for those who still believe that all it takes to quit the slums is a little guts and drive, I recommend the writings of James Baldwin, Claude Brown, Ralph Ellison and Charles Wright among others. To break out of rural poverty or the urban ghetto requires a combination of human traits rare in any section of society. When we treat the poor as evil and insist they be thoroughly investigated before they can receive any welfare, we enrage the recipients, frustrate the goals of the program and multiply expenses by requiring a vast army of investigators.

At the heart of the bureaucratic problem of welfare for those in poverty lies the Aid for Dependent Children program (ADC). The magnitude of ADC is such that the way it works affects us all. Before they reach the age of eighteen one out of ten white children in our society will have been supported by ADC, and six out of ten nonwhite children. For many fatherless families, ADC is the principal source of income. This program, which many regard as the underpinning of our welfare system, has worked in the past and still works at present to destroy the initiative of those who want jobs and force the break-up of families.

Until 1962 the family of an unemployed man could not receive public assistance until he had deserted them. Those were the rules—the law of the land. Some of those laws have been modified, but at this moment an employed man who is working full-time cannot receive benefits for his children, even though his total earnings are less than the family next door on welfare. For example, a father of four working full-time at the minimum wage can, under the ADC program, increase his family income from roughly $200 to $250 a month by abandoning his family. On a less grand but intimately human level, at the present time in Boston some recipients of ADC are required to get written permission from their social worker—on the proper form naturally—before they can ask the newspaper and department store Santa Clauses for gifts for their children.

Other indications about the performance of welfare programs and the welfare bureaucracy cause equal concern. Recent data estimate that for every person on welfare there is another who is eligible for the program but not participating. Many of these do not know the programs exist. Others are unwilling to make the sacrifice of pride and privacy involved. Some young girls choose prostitution over welfare because the conditions and investigations necessary before they can get aid are so destructive to their pride. And these are but a few indicators of how the present program functions.

A private industrial firm engaged in the production of cars would be out of business quickly if a substantial number of its automobiles exploded on the road. The welfare programs of the federal government are supposed to help citizens find their way in society; instead, they break families apart and contribute to the riots in our cities.

As an immediate priority we must substitute for these present welfare programs a series of strategies that aid the recipients in their own battle against poverty. Most present programs are not just obsolescent; they are dangerous. Our goal is to make the self-evident truth of equality physically self-evident to all here and now by helping people to achieve pride and dignity for themselves. The test of our strategies should be that they hold families together and treat all children as what they are: small, vulnerable portions of our country's future.

Several different strategies are persuasively advocated to aid individuals, families and children. We should probably try at least two or three of these. The one that works best now may work less well later; one that works in Appalachia may not work in Detroit. We should remain flexible—free to compare, test and change our minds.

One important part of helping people to help themselves could be a family allowance. With family allowance, payments are made to everyone in America for each child. The United States is the only industrial democracy in the western world that does not have such a family allowance program. Canada for example now provides each child under ten with six dollars a month. It seems to me reasonable that the United States should adopt some similar form of payment. Though all families in America would receive the allowance, the more affluent would pay most of it back in taxes.

Since all families would receive family allowance as a right of citizenship, those most in need would have no cause to feel separate or worthless. When all partake of an equal right, we have started to erase the boundary between "we" and "they." The extra money would work to hold families together since it starts at the moment of maximum strain, when a new child is added to the family. And finally, since the added money would go to everyone, social workers who now spend their time investigating whether a family is poor enough to receive aid would have their time and energies freed for counseling and guidance.

Whenever power and money are involved, certain checks and safeguards are necessary. There are always a few who are ready to cheat, to take advantage outside the law. At present, most income tax returns are checked on the basis of machine random sampling. This would seem an adequate way to monitor any aid program. Again all parts of society would be treated the same.

An argument often advanced against family allowance is that population control is one of the world's most urgent needs and a family allowance will increase the number of children born. There is no statistical evidence that this is so. The American and Canadian birth rates have risen and fallen at the same rate; yet Canada has had a family allowance and we have not. I think that the argument that roughly one hundred and twenty more dollars a year would encourage families to have unwanted children is again evidence of the unrecognized premise that the poor are the dark side of ourselves.

The ill, the elderly, the working mothers with small children and those unable to work for other reasons must be aided to escape poverty. Again the goals of the program must be kept in mind—to create true equality of opportunity and help people build dignity for themselves. Poverty will not be abolished until each individual has as a basic right an income that will keep him above the poverty level.

Mothers heading households with small children are particularly in need of money for sustenance. Modern psychology and ancient wisdom join in stressing the importance of love and attention in a baby's first years. There is no substitute for a mother's love. But there is no substitute for food either. Society should never force a woman to choose between an unattended child and a starving one. We need a strategy that will provide enough income to keep all above the poverty level and at the same time nourish the initiative and increase the benefits of those working productively.

SERVICES

A final word about services such as family planning, guidance, counseling, medical aid, technical training. Many of these programs are worthwhile and have dedicated people working in them. But the poor in their need are often unaware that programs exist to help them. There is marked contrast between the flood of information directed at the rest of the public about services and the trickle that reaches the poor. Banks, loan associations, savings bonds and investment funds direct expensive advertising campaigns at the affluent about how they should manage their money or spend their time. Industries and states employ highly paid Washington staffs to instruct them on how to obtain government funds. The poor are lucky if they hear a garbled report from a friend. The communications industry should be encouraged to move aggressively into this gap, and devise strategies by which those living in poverty learn what services are available to them and that they can accept these services without loss of pride because they are available as a matter of right.

In the field of services the strategy may again be the creation of Special Purpose Corporations, this time on a local rather than a national level like URBX. Such corporations could imaginatively dispense services that have been flattened into unattractiveness beneath the leaden weight of federal and local bureaucracy. These corporations could also coordinate to make certain that the standards of antipoverty services are nationally the same. Brutal local standards that callously shift the hard-core poor from one area to another in the nation must be stopped. The efficiency of American industry in producing superior consumer goods has become a world legend. With the proper incentives and control, special corporations (both profit and nonprofit) in the private sector should be able to help produce superior people.

SPORTS

It is not enough to just take care of the financial needs of the underprivileged young men and women. We need a program that constructively harnesses the energies of youth to the pursuit of excellence—not just on a crash basis in the summer but all year round. I am convinced that a vast program of competitive amateur sports would be of great benefit not merely to the underprivileged but to the nation as a whole. Nothing convinces a man of his own worth more rapidly than excellence in athletics. But millions of youngsters are denied adequate coaching, facilities and incentives for sports because they do not attend college or belong to those few sports clubs restricted to the wealthy. It is a sad fact of life in today's America that unless a young man or woman is able to go to college or a good high school, he or she may never be able to achieve their full potential in sports. We have no idea how many Althea Gibsons are walking around our streets, unable to find a ball, much less a racket or a court.

A few years ago when I became convinced that sports might provide one answer to the long, hot summer, I got all the Ivy League colleges to agree to keep their sports facilities open all summer to everyone. Many of these facilities in cities such as New Haven or Boston were located close to the areas of greatest need. The institutions set only one minor condition on their agreement. They wanted the federal government to insure them against unreasonable lawsuits that might be brought against them by those injured on their property.

I personally carried the request for this small sum to President Johnson so that the program could get started. I was told the funds were not available. The money came to less than we spend in one hour in Vietnam. And the facilities were immediately available. Yet the present administration insists it is totally committed to the war on poverty.

The ancient Greeks fully realized the value of athletics

in society. Plato devoted much space in his *Republic* to the importance of athletic training. The Olympic games were solemn and memorable occasions throughout the then known world, and other events were even dated by them. In the middle of the Peloponnesian War a truce was declared so that the games could be held.

Today sports are recognized as an integral part of education, not just because of their contribution to the individual's physical well-being, but also because through sport the individual finds basic self-expression and develops the ability to contribute with others toward common goals. Another benefit is the gain of that difficult-to-define but universally recognized and respected concept of sportsmanship and fair play. In our industrial society Americans are enjoying more and more leisure; at this time sports have become increasingly important to all of us, even to those who only enjoy them vicariously on television.

The Soviet Union, quoting the Russian psychologist Pavlov: "The joy of motion is the joy of life," has made sports into a national way of life. Fifty million people are registered members of government sporting clubs. Every year in July national games are held and athletes from all over the Soviet Union compete. From the best of these they select those who will go on to the Olympics. There are three levels of schools devoted entirely to sport. And a vast and much publicized building program for stadiums and gymnasiums.

Here in America we have not even made the few facilities we have, available to everyone. And these facilities are not only deficient in number but also in quality.

This is particularly true in low-income areas where the need is greatest, both in farm communities and in the urban ghetto. (Historically many of our finest athletes have come from these areas.) In some Olympic sports the nation actually possesses no facility at all. Our only year-round 400-meter speed-skating track was recently torn down to make a parking lot. We have but one bobsled run (for which New York State picks up the deficit) and no luge run. And we have no national organization that would enable all amateur athletes in individual and team sports to compete with each other in regional and national games. We are, in fact, neglecting the whole man. This applies not just to the poor but to all of us.

A National Sports Foundation would strengthen amateur sports in America today and provide facilities and coaching for every American. This foundation would not merely hand out money, but be an operating organization responsible for the development, construction and maintenance of sports facilities as well as the training and provision of coaching. Somewhat similar in organization and operation to the Red Cross or the National Academy of Sciences, the foundation would receive initial grants from both the federal government and the private sector. Thereafter its budget would be provided by endowment and financed in part by a portion of the revenues from the TV rights and ticket sales to various of its athletic events. I need hardly stress the benefit from such a foundation and program to the nation as a whole in future Olympic games.

The pursuit of excellence in any endeavor has always fascinated me, from broad jumping to taking thought.

So much energy, time and self-discipline are required. By making sports available to everybody we open up a truly democratic arena in which all can try their skills against each other. We will even have surpassed the ancient Greeks, for in their games neither slaves nor non-Greeks could compete. Nor were women permitted to watch—a rule that would be somewhat impossible to enforce today. Perhaps we have advanced more than we know.

ART, HISTORY AND UNITY

In the old days in America, the small-town days—whose image we carry recessed in our minds as a refuge from today's urban nightmare—the village had a central square. On the green grass of the square would stand a cannon or other monument commemorating the dead of the Revolutionary War or the Civil War. About the square would stand the town hall, the church, the library, the few stores and the bank.

Business, government, a sense of the past and the needs of the mind and spirit were seen grouped in visible, local unity. All this has utterly vanished. City Hall is miles away, stores are supermarkets affiliated with national chains, the bank functions by computer, there are no monuments, and for many the church has become non-operative. There is no place we can go when we seek spiritual refreshment, either through knowledge of our cultural historic past or through the excitement of our artistic present. True, there are museums, theaters, and galleries in the downtown areas of the city. But for most these are too far away, unknown, open at the wrong times and far too expensive. In our neglect of the whole man we have forgotten his cultural and spiritual needs. In this area many in the suburbs are as impoverished as those in urban and rural poverty areas. We need places in the cities, suburbs, and rural countryside, where men and women can go when they wish to spend some time in communion with art, history or whatever will refresh their spirits. We need places like the free libraries the generosity of Andrew Carnegie established in so many small towns across the land.

Recently in France, André Malraux, the Minister of Culture, has had great success with the development of vest-pocket cultural centers scattered about the country. These small, excitingly designed buildings serve neighborhoods rather than cities as a whole. They house traveling art and historical exhibitions and serve visiting theatrical groups, thus making it possible for residents in various areas to enjoy something of the richness and grandeur of present and past French culture.

I believe we should have such centers scattered about our own cities and countryside. They should be designed by outstanding architects so that the buildings themselves would produce a feeling of the excitement and richness of American creativity. Inside the buildings would be space for art exhibits, both permanent and visiting, and also for pictures produced by local talent. There would be space for historical exhibits, the artifacts of our past, to which all our people have contributed. There would be taped libraries of music with earphones so that people could listen to what they wished as the mood fell on them. Some of the centers could contain areas where on small screens short motion pictures could be shown, explaining aspects of our historical and cultural past. There would be a place for sculpture, a reading room, a limited library with facilities for the electronic search of central catalogues. The centers would also contain a small auditorium where local groups could meet and visiting and local theatrical companies perform.

In painting, theater and music, the American contribution to world culture is much stronger and more vital than many realize. There is a value to be gained from actual contact with a work of art, whether a painting on the wall or a play on the stage, that no television image can duplicate. To bring more people in contact with the spiritual and cultural achievements of all mankind cannot help but broaden our sense of direction and increase the quality of our lives and dreams for the future. Nor is it chauvinism to believe we would all benefit from more frequent exposure to the art and culture of our own past and present.

EDUCATION

Studies of poverty from Appalachia to Watts all identify better education as a vital step in the rise of the individual from the underculture. The high school dropout has become a favorite study for reporters and caseworkers, though unfortunately little has been done to help him. It is understood now that families composed of dropouts produce more dropouts and so the fatal cycle of poverty continues in ever-widening circles. At the start of education, programs such as Headstart have sought to prepare the disadvantaged for school, although here again bureaucrats seem to have been following their own ideas of how a program should operate rather than setting process goals and testing to see what method succeeded in reaching a given goal.

Unfortunately better education has often been made to seem a panacea for all the evils of the ghetto. But the problem is complex, and better education is merely one point of attack. Housing, jobs, an end to discrimination are equally important parts of the total battle. As has been stressed all along, there is no way to get through our domestic crisis cheaply by adopting just this or just that part of the program. The best education possible can accomplish little if individual energy is not released by the stimulus of environment and opportunity.

Education by itself without other benefits and opportunities can deepen the alienation of the underculture member from society. The availability of a job is a critical aspect of the individual's escape from poverty. Yet at present for underculture members the operation of society gives the lie to the publicly preached values of education. A Negro who stays in high school and finishes has less of a chance, far less of a chance, to get a job than the white who drops out. In the under-twenty age group 9 per cent of the white high school dropouts are unemployed, but in the same age group 13 per cent of the Negro high school *graduates* are unemployed.

Whom are we kidding about the value of education?

Certainly not the young Negro. He can look about him and see the difference between our actions and words. We are deceiving ourselves because we want to believe the problem easier to solve than it really is. If only education can be improved and the poor persuaded to stay in school, we will be out of the woods. That is not true. The causes of our long, hot summers are revealed in statistics such as these which tell of hopes raised and then frustrated. No amount of riot training for the National Guard will remove these causes.

But as part of the process of change better education is vital. And there are aspects of the poverty problem where education can be immediately effective. To start the process of change in education is as difficult as in any other area. Educational bureaucracies are no more receptive to innovation than any other bureaucratic group, indeed sometimes they seem less so. And as they maneuver to block progress they spew out a particularly inky cloud of technical jargon.

There are problems of neighborhood control over education versus uniform standards, of obsolescent licensing standards for teachers, of de facto segregation, of money, of the bright student or the dull versus the average, of conflicting theory, of the new open-school program. And all of these questions are exacerbated because they deal with young children about whose welfare we passionately care.

As an example of how to form strategies to attack the educational problem, consider vocational education and the ways to improve it. Public vocational education in many of our cities is in shambles. Children are falling behind in skills and their IQ's dropping while they are promoted from grade to grade. We should forget debates about how things were best done in the past and formulate goals that deal with the present crisis.

One immediate, measurable goal of vocational education could be to train and find jobs for the unemployed nonwhite teenager. Last summer twenty-seven per cent of nonwhite teenagers were unemployed. Although the percentage is high, the total number is small—about six hundred thousand. All who read the papers or watch television will recognize the vital importance of this group. A nation that produced 8,604,726 cars last year should be able to train and find satisfying jobs for most of these six hundred thousand. But we must begin now. Within five years, if nothing is done, the number of unemployed nonwhite teenagers will grow to over one million. The time for action on this front is five minutes past twelve.

Public education alone cannot solve this problem. Most public schools close in the summer by bureaucratic fiat, reinforced by union regulations—a combination much more definite than any mere act of God. Vocational schools in most cities are neglected and obsolete. The subjects taught in such schools have nothing to do with either what the students want or the job market. And the potential students, frustrated by their early experience with education, and understanding all too well their lack of opportunity, must be skillfully led back and trained to use their own resources by an exciting and specially designed educational environment. They must have the latest sophisticated teaching aids and be taught by such dedicated individuals as those who once entered the domestic and foreign Peace Corps.

To benefit the target group without starting a new federal program these six hundred thousand teenagers should be educated and found jobs by a combination of private industry and Special Purpose Corporations. In the battle to change our urban environment the plants of the large and small corporations are the front lines. Industries should redesign their job categories, recruiting efforts and job-training programs to fit the needs of these six hundred thousand. Here the benefits discussed under tax policy come to the aid of the corporation.

During World War II, when it became necessary to use women in jobs formerly held by men, industry responded with the necessary training programs and job changes. This same type of initiative can be successful now. With government guidance and stimulation and the concerned help of thoughtful unionism, private industry should be able to train and employ large numbers of these teenagers.

As another strategy of attack, local Special Purpose Corporations could be formed to train and find jobs for this group. The potential students should be consulted about the sort of work they want in the same way that the average high school student is asked to determine, within limits, the type of major he wants to take. This group with less experience of education and the job market will need more guidance. But the principle of individual choice remains basic.

Such Special Corporations will have a double function.

Not only will they train and find jobs for the unemployed, but they will also set the standard of excellence by which other vocational schooling, both in public education and in industry, can be measured. For years the privately endowed university, such as Yale or Harvard, has been the standard against which public universities measured themselves. These Special Purpose Corporations will provide the same type of standards for vocational education. Competition between various parts of our society in providing education is one of the strategies by which total improvement in education can be gained.

I think of education as property—a private piece of mental land from which each citizen draws nourishment, income and satisfaction in his moments of leisure. We are all born with a share of this property. To deprive a person of his property against his will has been recognized since prehistory as a most serious crime. We must make certain that we as a society do not commit this crime. We harm all of us when we do.

THE LARGER PERSPECTIVE

The initiative to bring about change in our national life rests ultimately with the President. Others can make suggestions or organize breakthroughs in specific areas and carry out local strategies and inventions. But the energy for a thorough attack upon our domestic crisis lies in the White House, just as does the basic initiative for war and peace. The President must lead the nation in whatever campaign is launched to improve our domestic environment. But the President also needs help.

After World War II, to aid the President in dealing with the world beyond American shores, the National Security Council was created as part of the executive office of the President. Its small staff, most of it free from the burden of civil service and responsible directly to the President, initiates and follows through the strategies and programs affecting the United States abroad. The National Security Council draws information, recommendations and ideas from all federal departments that have international responsibilities such as Defense, State, Treasury and Commerce and provides a mechanism by which the President can make decisions in the field of foreign affairs. The relationship of the council to the President and the prestige of its White House location enable the President to gather around him some of the finest brains and special talents in the nation to aid him in the formulation of foreign policy.

No such personal staff exists to help the President initiate and control strategies and programs for what is now the nation's number-one problem—our domestic crisis. He must deal with the many departments and agencies from Agriculture through the Health, Education and Welfare either by himself or on an ad hoc basis. The Bureau of the Budget tries to bring some sense out of the chaos, but in spite of the ability of its staff, this budgetary control is essentially negative—it can stop bad programs but has a hard time initiating good ones.

The President urgently needs a small staff modeled

along the lines of the National Security Council to help him battle our domestic crisis. An elite group, located in the executive offices of the President and responsible to the President alone, it could help provide the generative force and control the President needs in his direction of the vast changes necessary in our environment.

Americans know something is wrong. In Vietnam and our cities, what we are doing bears little relation to what we wish to do. Everywhere events turn against us. The government has lost control. Unless we take drastic action the situation will soon be very much worse. But the administration seems to have a fatal inability—and I use the word "fatal" advisedly, for the inability could be just that—to admit that any program it has espoused could be inadequate, or even worse, plain wrong.

Formerly, before change began to occur with such frightening speed, we could afford the luxury of not seeing or admitting errors; we had spaces of time between the recognition of crisis and the need for decisive action —there were, for instance, two and a half years between Pearl Harbor and D-Day. Today events race faster. To survive Vietnam and our domestic revolution we need to begin the process of change now.

VII

A COMMITMENT
TO CHANGE

W e approach the end of our brief look at America's present crisis. We began with the scientific revolution, showing how this seminal fact of life on most of the globe today was still largely unrecognized. The scientific revolution works as an invisible hand behind a broad spectrum of events—from such simple disasters as the *Torrey Canyon* and thalidomide to the revolution in our national strategy and the decay of our domestic environment. Mismanagement, shortsightedness, resistance to change and other human failings have compounded the chaos about us. But the basic causes have been the revolutionary changes created by science in machines, systems and society. Instead of making science work for us we have been struck and battered by unexpected results. And if we continue as we are, worse, much worse, lies ahead.

We have examined in detail the two principal aspects of our crisis now: military strategy, with specific emphasis on the war in Vietnam, and the revolution in our domestic life. In Vietnam we have lost sight of our national objectives and let what started as a limited war expand in time, cost and effort. We have ended up killing more people and fighting far longer than we had planned, and the added death and destruction so transform the fabric of Vietnamese society that they make impossible the attainment of the objectives for which we entered the war. At the same time this excess of violence poisons our domestic life.

The cities have been viewed not in isolation but as a product of the total system of our national environment. A change in fertilizers and agricultural machinery becomes part of the chain that leads to violence in the streets. Poverty, discrimination, bad housing, a growing population, pollution, obsolete political structures and substandard education are all strands of the urban crisis. The cities themselves lack the authority and strength to deal with the crisis. The federal government is rigid and inflexible, often inflaming the very evils it is supposed to cure. The magnitude of the problem demands abandoning old ways of thought and employing the knowledge and methods of science to free human energy and produce solutions of a virtually revolutionary nature.

Science progresses through change, through trial and error, through the rigid testing of new ideas and solutions. We must be prepared to advance our society in the same manner; we must examine a social problem such as the organization of our cities or a mechanical problem such as the pollution of our rivers and be prepared to try several different radical solutions. We must not be afraid to be sometimes wrong. We must test our solutions constantly so that we can concentrate our efforts on those which prove the most productive. To this process of change everyone must contribute, since everyone will be affected.

Testing will be an important part of any solution of our problems. The scientists in the proposed Manhattan Project II and the administrators of such strategies as URBX must be willing to try different solutions in different cities and test them against each other; in fact the whole government must adopt such an experimental approach. Leaders must be willing to listen to people as to how various strategies are working. All of us, from the ghettos to the most affluent suburbs, should be able to test in our lives what works best for us.

Science has also provided us with important concepts to help us handle our environment. We often fail to use these and continue to think in traditional ways. A key concept is that of the system: seeing a problem as composed of a number of interacting parts. This leap in the thinking process will make new solutions possible.

For example, in trying to solve the problems of pollution we still continue to think of man in the traditional way as a consumer. In point of scientific fact man is no more a consumer than a cow, a tree or a river. We are part of a process; we are processors. We take in certain forms of energy, we use certain tools and we create certain products and leave certain wastes. We alter or modify our environment; we do not consume.

Once we stop thinking of ourselves as consumers and start thinking of ourselves as modifiers we start to look at our environment with a present eye. The eggshell around our breakfast egg when thrown on the ground breaks down in a short period of time to nourish the soil. Might it not be equally important that the carton in which the eggs are packaged be made to do the same? Such a carton would cost more to design and make, but the present buyer of eggs is paying part of the expense of his carton in higher taxes to finance garbage disposal. Perhaps a better way would be to provide incentives to the manufacturer to make the carton differently, so that it, like the eggshell, builds rather than contaminates the total system of our urban environment. This is a small example, but one that illustrates the range of possibilities that open when we begin to use the concepts of science to effect changes in our environment and our lives.

In addition to intellectual concepts, science has given us the necessary tools to attack the problems around us. The yearly rise in our gross national product now equals the total yearly GNP of the 1930's. This vast wealth is available for the solution of our domestic problems, but this abundance, given us by our technology and our machines, we are expending in Vietnam rather than on ourselves and our friends.

We have the high-speed electronic calculators and other data-processing equipment with which to stimulate problems and compare the progress of different experiments. We have air conditioning and high-speed elevators to enable us to live, if we wish, in climates and in vertical stacks impossible before. We have instantaneous communications and sophisticated weaponry that could be put at the disposal of a U.N. police force. Yet these and many other similar tools are either unused, or even worse, misused.

Above all, science has given us time. The work week has been continually shortening since the close of World War II. We all have more leisure. We can budget this gift of time in a variety of ways: in sports, watching television, teaching our children, or politics. By politics I mean citizen participation in changing the social environment around us. The cry that more citizens should get interested in politics is an old one. In the past the legitimate answer of many has been: I don't have time. Men were involved with their jobs, women with their children and household chores.

This is changing. More and more people—and women have often been the pioneers in this—are finding they have time for politics. We are moving back toward the concept shared by Plato and the early American settlers that politics was an important part of the life of the whole man. As Plato wrote in his *Republic*: "The penalty that good men pay for not being interested in politics is to be governed by men worse than themselves." The scientific revolution has given us all more time for politics.

A WORLD OF CHANGE

All the strategies, inventions and solutions discussed in this book mean change. Traditionally men fear change. They like order in their lives, routines, established facts, a feeling of measured progress toward generally recognized goals. No matter how bad things are now, we have a tendency to cling to them for fear change will prove worse. This is the course we have been following: To let things be. Unfortunately we do not have a true choice: to change or not to change. For though we can decide to continue as we are, our actions keep changing the world about us at an increasing rate. Two results of such unplanned, haphazard change are Vietnam and our domestic crisis. In addition, when we have moved to try solving post-scientific-revolution problems with old ideas and concepts, far from improving conditions around us we have often made them worse.

Sometimes a phrase is heard so often that the truth behind it is masked. "We live in times of change" is such a phrase. We do not live in times of change. We live in change. Change is the constant of our lives. To say that we live in times of change presupposes that we are moving from a period of stability in the past toward a new period of stability in the future. I do not believe that at any time in the foreseeable future we will again live in a world without change—or one in which change is so gradual as to be undisturbing. I doubt, moreover, that the old days were as free of change as, looking backward, we like to imagine them to have been.

To move toward the unknown at our present accelerated rate is frightening. Many of the problems we face do seem almost beyond the boundaries of understanding and solution. Animals faced with problems beyond their capacity either curl up in a ball and hide or viciously begin to rend and claw whatever is closest. In our reactions to the problems posed by Vietnam and our domestic crisis we can see parts of such behavior. "Let's turn tail and pull out" or "Let's bomb them back to the Stone Age" are both examples of such solutions.

All around us are the human examples of the alarming effects of change. A man invests his life savings in a house and sees the neighborhood start to decay. A man learns a particular specialty or trade and as he reaches his mature years, society's need for that specialty or trade vanishes. Children and parents read different books, watch different films, have different values. There always was a "generation gap," but as change accelerates, that gap widens. With work becoming less important, politics changing, the nuclear threat increasing and the environment decaying, men find it difficult to be sure who they are. And unless a man is sure who he is and what he stands for he cannot transmit values to his children.

Conditions of constant surprise and change describe life on a frontier. The scientific revolution has placed us all on the frontier. We all live in change. This time there is no safe eastern seaboard where those who wish can remain. To accomplish our individual and national purposes we have to keep ourselves and our institutions flexible and responsive to rapid change.

To live on a frontier is to exist both in challenge and in opportunity. Crisis which brings out the best in most men will bring out the worst in some—we have only to look about us in America today to test the truth of this. However, I think it no mere coincidence that the two great Presidents of this nation's middle period, Jackson and Lincoln, were both from the frontier. Not fearing change in their own lives, they were able to initiate, control and guide profound changes in America.

Choices on a frontier are brutal and hard. I do not wish to glamorize them. But I believe that as a nation we have always been at our best in time of crisis, on the frontier. In any period of time there have been people among us who accepted change and challenge as a way of life. For one generation it may be the frontier scout, in the next the entrepreneur, in another the immigrant, in another the social reformer, in still another the physicist. We all need in our lives at least a portion of the commitment to change shown by such men. We need to accept that tomorrow will be different. Whether it will be better or worse depends on ourselves.

CHANGE IN INSTITUTIONS

In addition to a commitment to change in our own lives we need to build flexibility into the strategies and inventions we create to deal with foreign affairs and our urban crisis. The framers of our Constitution were acutely conscious of this need to provide an orderly means for change and growth. Having just passed through the Revolution, with the frontier all around them, they understood change. Their debates, letters and articles show how clearly most of them realized that they could see only the dim outlines of our country's future. They were aware that institutions created with the best will in the world could become tyrannical almost overnight. They wanted a document that could stand the test of change.

Their solution is well known: a system of checks and balances, with the power of the Executive, Congress and Judiciary in balance against each other. Their governmental architecture has withstood the test of time. As the nation changed, each branch of the government has clashed with each other and the system has adjusted itself. Yet except for the Civil War, change has occurred inside the process of democratic government.

This system devised by the founding fathers is analogous to the system of scientific experiment. Recognizing change as a constant, science provides that hypotheses and theories be checked and rechecked against known data. Different men or different groups of men will hold different theories about the nature of our environment. But over a period of time, in competition with each other, the more accurate theory slowly displaces the others.

American law, too, provides for change and flexibility. If a man disagrees with the law of the land he adopts an adversary position. He takes his view of the right before the courts and fights for it. Those who disagree with him battle equally hard upon the other side. At the end, a solution is reached, not by fiat, but by conflict within a framework. And that solution in turn becomes modified by other cases as other men attack or defend aspects of the law.

In our laws, in science, in the Constitution, we see how planned conflict built into a social system provides for flexibility and change. But as we discovered when we looked at our urban crisis, there are no such provisions for conflict and change built into the federal bureaucracy, or the city-state relationship. Those who designed the departments of Agriculture, of Labor, of Health, Education, and Welfare believed they had hold of a social good that would remain constant. They designed into the system no method of conflict or change. That is why the strategies discussed in this book to solve our present crisis have for the most part advocated actions outside of the federal bureaucracy and why such inventions and strategies must have designed into them methods for adversary positions and change.

The successful private industry is also aware that it operates in a system of change, checks and balances. These include everything from the threat of product obsolescence to the pressure of competitors, the demands of labor unions and the condition of the money market. Some private industries do stultify and become as rigid as any government bureaucracy, but those that do soon find their profits dwindling. Companies that manufacture wagon wheels do not prosper in the age of the automobile. A governmental bureaucracy, on the other hand, can continue to produce wagon wheels in a jet age and be relatively free from pressure to change. It is this sensitivity to change of the well-run private corporation that would make private and Special Purpose Corporations so useful in the battle against our domestic crisis.

CRISIS AND COMMITMENT

I began this book by saying that our crisis was also our challenge. I do not see the administration accepting this challenge. Instead it seems to me that despair has become the common denominator of too many actions taken by ourselves and our country. If we had to wait until we had solved all our problems before we could start to hope, I would be right in there despairing myself. Our problems are vast and complex. In solving some we create others. If our environment would not begin to improve until a great many changes had been thoroughly completed, it might already be too late.

We do not have to wait that long. The instant we begin to turn this country around from the past toward the future we begin to alter the environment in which we live. At the instant of commitment to change, we begin to move from crisis now to hope now. I do not mean it will be easy, or that problems will vanish, or that there will not sometimes be darkness at noon; but the atmosphere about us will lighten.

We created the equipment that won World War II; we developed nuclear energy; we put shattered Europe back on its feet with the Marshall Plan. When we choose we can not only move mountains, we can move nations —which is much harder. But we have neither chosen nor been offered a choice.

We need change now. The size of our commitment should be measured by the challenge of our crisis, not by some leftover yardsticks from our past. We are a great nation. We do not have to live this way: in error abroad and squalor at home. We can alter our present and control our future. We can choose. We can commit ourselves to an effort, an ideal, a dream.

I believe that children walking home from school a thousand years from now, speaking languages as yet unheard, will turn to one another and say, "America, in the years when they fulfilled their Revolution—that was the time to be alive." I know this is a dream. I believe this dream is shared by most of us. And that our strength will make our dream our future.

ABOUT THE AUTHOR

JAMES M. GAVIN, orphaned before he was two, enlisted in the Army at seventeen years of age, and from the ranks won a competitive examination to West Point. A paratrooper, he led four parachute assaults into Europe, planned the airborne invasion for D-Day, and became the youngest American division commander since the Civil War. Paradoxically, though an early and thoughtful critic of the Vietnamese war, it was he who created the sky cavalry or helicopter tactics being used in Vietnam today. In 1954 General Gavin became Chief of Plans, and of Research and Development for the Army. His outspoken concern over the policy of massive nuclear retaliation at the expense of a more flexible strategy led to his resignation from the Army in 1958. At that time he joined Arthur D. Little, Inc., a management consultant firm located in Cambridge, Massachusetts—one of whose major interests is America's domestic environment. In 1960 he was appointed ambassador to France by President John F. Kennedy. On his return from Paris he rejoined Arthur D. Little, Inc., where he is now chairman of the board.

General Gavin has written three books and numerous magazine articles. His writings are known for their brilliant and courageous treatment of both military and domestic problems.

ARTHUR T. HADLEY was both White House correspondent and Military Affairs editor for *Newsweek*. He is the author of five books.